Science Everywhere

3

SENIOR AUTHORS

Les Asselstine
Rod Peturson

Brendene Barkley
Cynthia Clarke
Sharron Cooke
Dick Coombs
Margaret Gibson
Brian Herrin
Marcia Klein
Elizabeth LeLacheur
Linda Manson
Bob Piccott
Carla Pieterson
Pamela Quigg
Brenda Shynal
Bryan Szumlas
Anna Totten

CONSULTANT: SCIENTIFIC ACCURACY

Arthur Prudham

HARCOURT
BRACE
CANADA

Harcourt Brace & Company, Canada
Toronto • Orlando • San Diego • London • Sydney

Canadian Cataloguing in Publication Data
Asselstine, Les, 1943-
    Science everywhere 3

ISBN 0-7747-0556-6

1. Science — Juvenile literature. 2. Technology — Juvenile literature.
I. Peturson, Rod, 1952-   . II. Title.

Q163.A873 1999   500   C99-931113-1

Project Manager: Julie Kretchman
Writers/Editors: Joanne Close, Todd Mercer, Lynn Pereira,
    Elizabeth Salomons
Editorial Assistants: Ian Nussbaum, Brett Savory
Manager of Editorial Services: Nicola Balfour
Senior Production Editor: Karin Fediw
Production Editors: Dawn Hunter, Mary Knittl,
    Margot Miller, Carol Martin
Permissions Coordinator: Patricia Buckley
Photo Researcher: Mary Rose MacLachlan
Production Manager: Sheila Barry
Production Coordinator: Tanya Mossa
Art Direction and Design: Sonya V. Thursby/Opus House Incorporated
Layout: Megan Byrne/Water Street Graphics, Steve Eby
Cover Image: Doug Armand/Tony Stone Images

Contents

Welcome to Science Everywhere!

Science can be found in nearly anything you see or do.
In *Science Everywhere* you will learn

- how plants grow and change
- how force make things move
- how to build strong, stable buildings
- what soil does for us

This book begins with Start-Up Science. In Start-Up
Science you will be introduced to magnets and
experiment to learn how magnets work.

Start-Up Science

Where do you see science in this picture?

In your science journal describe what you see in the picture. You can draw a picture, make a chart, or write a few sentences. Scientists keep notes of their observations. A science journal is a good place to keep your notes.

Let's get started! Make a title page for your science journal. Draw pictures of objects that have magnets in them. At the end of this unit you may want to add more objects after you learn more about magnets.

Stuck On You

Magnets are all around us. Look at this picture. Which objects have magnets? List them in your science journal.

In Getting Started you will look for magnets in everyday objects. In Let's Investigate you will find out which objects stick to a magnet.

GETTING STARTED

Look around you. What objects in your home and at school have magnets in them? Write a list of these objects in your science journal.

LET'S INVESTIGATE

Find out what sticks to a magnet.

1. Put the objects into two piles. In one pile put things you think will stick to a magnet. In the other pile put things you think will not stick to a magnet.

You will need
- a collection of objects
- a magnet

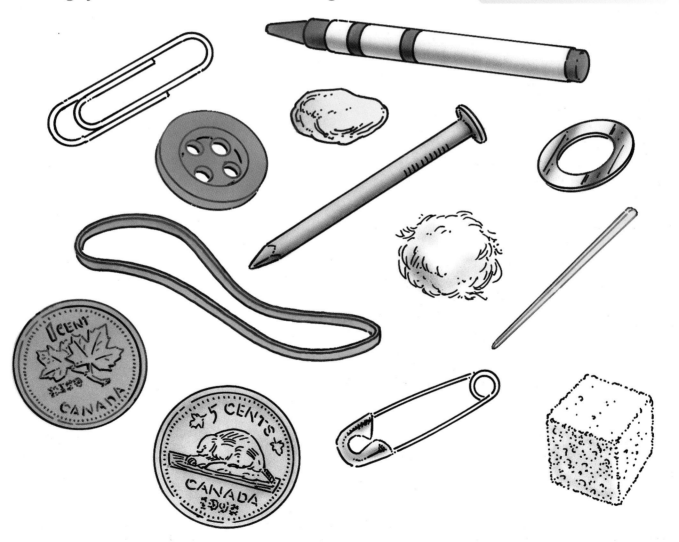

2. Test each object.

3. Make a chart. Write your results in it.

What Sticks to a Magnet?	
Things that stick to a magnet	Things that don't stick to a magnet

Reflect on Your Results

Magnets should never be put near electrical machines, such as computers and VCRs, because they can damage the equipment.

1. Look around the classroom. Choose an object you believe will stick to a magnet. Then, use a magnet to find out.

2. In which pile does a penny belong? In which pile does a nickel belong? Why? Test a few pennies and a few nickels. Do all pennies act the same way? Do all nickels act the same way? Why?

3. Write a sentence in your science journal describing what you discovered about magnets.

What Did You Learn?

1. Read the Information Station. List three things we use magnets for.

2. What kinds of objects does a magnet attract?

Magnets

A magnet is usually a piece of metal that pulls or attracts other metal objects toward it. Most magnets are made from iron or a metal that has iron in it. When something attracts a metal object, we call it magnetism.

There are many hidden magnets in your home. You may not see them, but they do a lot of work for you. There are hidden magnets in a washing machine, a vacuum cleaner, a radio, and even in a television. Computers use magnets to store information on floppy disks.

Sometimes an object looks as if it should stick to a magnet, but it doesn't. Think of a penny and a nickel. A nickel sticks to a magnet because the metal used to make the coin is attracted to magnets. A penny doesn't stick to a magnet because it is made of copper. Some metals, like copper, are not attracted to magnets.

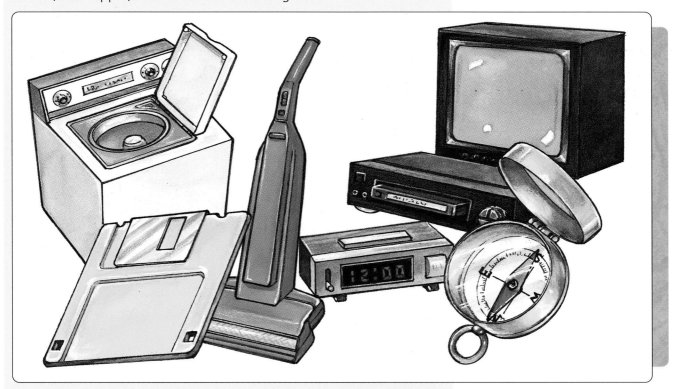

Magnetic Power

Some magnets are stronger than others. Some magnets are only strong enough to attract steel nails. Some are strong enough to pick up cars. Some are so strong, they can help electric trains move!

In Getting Started you will examine the strength of different types of magnets. In Let's Investigate you will test the strength of magnets. In Investigating Further you can use a graph to record the results of your investigation.

GETTING STARTED

Hold a magnet about 30 cm above a paper clip. How close will the magnet have to be to the paper clip to pick it up? Write your guess in your science journal. Slowly move the magnet closer to the paper clip. Repeat this with another magnet. Write your results in your science journal.

LET'S INVESTIGATE

Work with a partner to find the strongest magnet.

You will need
- 2 or more magnets of different shapes and sizes
- paper clips

◀ A magnet can pick up paper clips in a line. A magnet can pick up a bunch of paper clips.

Here are two ways you can test the strength of a magnet.

1. Choose a magnet. How many paper clips do you think it can pick up in the two different ways shown in the picture above? Write your guesses in your science journal.

2. Pick up a line of paper clips with the magnet. In your science journal write how many paper clips you picked up.

3. Pick up a bunch of paper clips with the magnet. In your science journal write how many paper clips you picked up.

4. Repeat steps 1 to 3 using the same magnet.

5. Repeat steps 1 to 3 using a different magnet.

Reflect on Your Results

1. What did you discover about the two ways you can pick up paper clips using a magnet?

2. Which is the better way to pick up paper clips? Why?

3. Which was the strongest magnet? How do you know?

What Did You Learn?

1. Did the size or shape of the magnet affect the number of paper clips it could lift? Explain your answer in your science journal.

Discovering Magnets

Where did magnets first come from?
A long time ago people noticed that
some metals stuck to certain special
rocks. These rocks are called
lodestone. Lodestone is a natural
magnet. Nails and paper clips will
stick to lodestone just as they stick to
the magnets in your classroom. The
word *magnet* may have come from
Magnesia, a place in ancient Greece.

▲ lodestone

INVESTIGATING FURTHER

Using a Graph

Make a pictograph to show the number of paper clips
each magnet held. Give the graph a title and labels.
Compare your graph with a classmate's graph. Why
might you each have different results?

For help making a
pictograph, see the Toolkit
on page 243.

Poles Apart

Magnets are used to attract things. What are the magnets attracted to in this picture?

In **Getting Started** you will guess what happens when two magnets are held near one another. In **Let's Investigate** you will find out how magnets affect one another.

GETTING STARTED

What would happen if two magnets were held near one another? Would they pull together or would they push apart? Write your answer in your science journal.

LET'S INVESTIGATE

In the first part of this activity, you'll find out what happens when two magnets are placed together. In the second part you'll make your own magnet and use it in an experiment.

PART 1: PUSH OR PULL?

1. Place two bar magnets end to end. What do you notice? Write your observations in your science journal.

2. Turn one magnet around. Place this end against the other magnet. What do you notice?

Reflect on Your Results

1. How did the magnets act differently when you turned one around?

INFORMATION STATION

Attraction

When you put one end or pole of a magnet near a pole of another magnet, you may have felt them pull together, or attract. Or, you may have felt the magnets push away or repel each other. The two poles of a magnet are called the north pole and the south pole. Sometimes they are called the N-pole and the S-pole. All magnets act in the same way: the two poles that are the same will push away from each other, while the two poles that are different will pull together.

You will need
- several small paper clips
- a bar magnet
- 1 large steel nail
- some string

PART 2: MAKE YOUR OWN MAGNET

1. Stroke the nail about 50 times with the bar magnet. Always stroke the nail in the same direction and with the same end of the magnet.

2. Touch the nail to a small paper clip. What happens? What have you made?

3. Tie a string around the middle of the nail and hold the string so that the nail is hanging in the air. Slowly bring the N-pole of the magnet close to one end of the nail. What happens? Now slowly bring the N-pole close to the other end of the nail. Write your observations in your science journal.

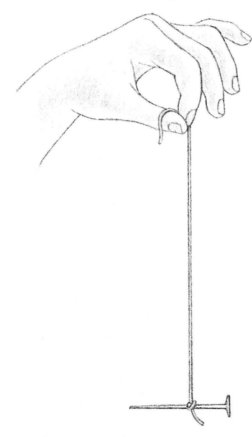

4. Repeat step 3, but this time slowly bring the S-pole of the magnet close to each end of the nail.

5. Repeat step 1. Then, try to pick up as many paper clips as you can with one end of the nail. Try it with the other end. How many paper clips did you pick up with each end of the nail? Write your observations in your science journal.

6. Look around the classroom. What else can you make into a magnet? Write your observations in your science journal.

Reflect on Your Results

1. What happened when you brought the N-pole of the magnet close to each end of the nail?

2. What happened when you brought the S-pole of the magnet close to each end of the nail?

3. Discuss what you learned with a classmate.

What Did You Learn?

1. In your science journal write a letter to someone in your family, telling them what you discovered about the north and south poles of magnets.

SCIENTISTS IN ACTION

William Gilbert was born in 1544 and worked as a doctor in London, England. In 1600 he published an important book on magnetism. In his book Gilbert described how he stroked steel rods with lodestone, a natural magnet, to magnetize them. His experiment is similar to Let's Investigate, where you magnetized a nail. You are now a Scientist in Action! Gilbert also concluded that the earth acts like a giant magnet. You can read more about this in Science in Our Lives.

SCIENCE IN OUR LIVES

Long ago, people discovered that they could find north by floating a thin piece of lodestone in a bowl of water. The north pole on the lodestone pointed to the magnetic North Pole in the Arctic Ocean. The south pole on the lodestone pointed to the magnetic South Pole on Antarctica. In fact, this is how the first compasses were made. Today compasses look different, but they still contain a magnet.

▲ a lodestone compass

▲ a modern compass

INVESTIGATING FURTHER

Try Tapping It

Tap your nail magnet on the table 10 times. Try to pick up a paper clip with your nail magnet. What does tapping a magnet do to its strength?

Passing Through

In **Stuck on You**, you learned about which objects are attracted to magnets and which aren't. In **Magnetic Power** you learned that some magnets are stronger than others. You have also seen that magnets can be used to hold things to certain surfaces, such as notes to a refrigerator door.

In **Getting Started** you will examine how magnetic force passes through certain materials. In **Let's Experiment** you will guess which materials a magnet's force will pass through and then test them.

GETTING STARTED

Look at the picture on page 22. A magnet will not pick up a piece of paper, but magnets hold these pieces of paper to a refrigerator. Why do you think this happens? What else will a magnet hold to a fridge door?

LET'S EXPERIMENT

Work with a partner to find out which materials a magnet's strength will pass through.

1. Work with a classmate. Make a chart like this in your science journal.

Things a Magnet's Strength Will Pass Through		
I think a magnet will pass through	I found a magnet will pass through	I found a magnet won't pass through

You will need
- a strong magnet
- paper clips
- paper
- cardboard
- aluminum foil
- spoons (plastic and metal)
- pie plates (glass, steel, and paper)

2. Spread some paper clips on a table. Choose a material to place over them.

3. Will the magnet be able to attract the paper clips through the material? Make a guess and write your answer in your chart.

4. Test your answer and write the result in your chart.

5. Choose and test several materials. Write your results in your chart each time.

Reflect on Your Results

1. How true were your guesses? What clues helped you?

2. Which materials, if any, did you have trouble with? Why?

3. Compare your chart with a classmate's chart. How are they alike? How are they different?

What Did You Learn?

1. Name the materials a magnet can attract things through.

2. Name the materials a magnet cannot attract things through.

3. Write a sentence in your science journal that describes what materials a magnet is able to pass through. Write another sentence that describes what materials a magnet is not able to pass through.

INFORMATION STATION

Passing Through

A magnet will be more likely to attract an object if

- the magnet is strong
- the object is close
- there is nothing metal between the magnet and the object

Your paper clips probably seemed to stick to the cardboard because the magnet was attracting them through the cardboard. The paper clips probably did not appear to stick to the steel pie plate. The magnet could not attract them through the metal.

INVESTIGATING FURTHER

Will it Pass Through Water?

Does magnetism pass through water? Use a paper clip, a magnet, and a clear glass of water to find out. What did you do? What did you learn? Think of other materials magnetism may, or may not, pass through and test them. Write the results of your tests in your science journal and share your results with the rest of the class.

GROWING GREEN

Plants are amazing. They come in all shapes and sizes and colours. They don't need much to grow. They provide homes for many animals. On top of all that, some of them taste good.

Thousands of different plants grow in Canada. Some of the plants we use for food are shown here. Which ones do you recognize?

In this unit, you will see how plants grow. You will also look at all the important things plants do for us. Then you will look at all the places where plants keep food: in their roots, in their leaves, in their seeds, in their stems, and in their bulbs.

WILD IN THE SUPERMARKET

Some people grow their own vegetables, but most of us get our food from a supermarket.

In Getting Started you will talk about the kinds of plants you eat. In Let's Investigate you will play a guessing game with a mystery food. In Investigating Further you can find out more about what happens to a plant before it gets to your dinner table.

GETTING STARTED

What kinds of plants do you eat? With a partner, list all the foods in the picture on page 28 that come from plants. Then answer these questions together: What plant does each food in the picture come from? What part of the plant does each food come from?

Make a list of all the foods you have eaten so far today. How many came from plants? Make a class chart of all the plant foods your class has eaten today.

LET'S INVESTIGATE

Play a guessing game to learn more about foods that come from plants.

1. Bring a mystery food to class. (It must be a food that comes from a plant.) Don't show it to any of your classmates.
2. Put your mystery food in a paper bag.

You will need
- a mystery food from home
- a paper bag

Does your mystery food grow underground?

3. Let the others in your group ask questions about your mystery food and try to guess what it is. You must be able to answer each question by saying yes or no.

4. If your group members still can't guess what your mystery food is after 10 questions, show them what's inside your paper bag.

5. Take turns guessing each other's mystery foods.

Reflect on Your Results

1. What plant made the food you brought in?

2. Which part of the plant was it from?

3. Which questions helped you the most when you were guessing the mystery foods of the others in your group?

4. Which mystery food was the hardest to guess? Why?

INFORMATION STATION

▲ cotton

Plenty of Plants

Plants are important to us. They produce oxygen that we need to breathe. They also keep our soil in good shape so that more plants can grow. We can eat some plants, too.

We use plants for many other things as well. Furniture and buildings are often made of wood.

The books and magazines you read are all made of paper. Paper also comes from trees. Logs are cut into wood chips. These chips are heated with water and chemicals and sometimes bits of straw. This makes pulp. The pulp is taken to a paper mill where other materials are added to it. Then the pulp is rolled into paper and dried.

The cotton in some of our clothes comes from cotton plants. The flowers of these plants produce puffs of long white hairs. These hairs, or fibres, are picked and then spun into yarn. The yarn is woven into cloth. ▶

Rubber, like the kind used to make balloons and rubber balls, is made from the sap of rubber trees. The sap is removed from the trees, then cleaned and put in huge tubs. Chemicals are added to turn the liquid sap into a solid. The water is then squeezed out and the rubber is rolled into sheets which are hung up to dry. The sheets of rubber are then taken to factories where they are made into all sorts of useful products.

SCIENCE IN OUR LIVES

Preserving Food

Long before there were refrigerators, people dried food out to keep it from spoiling.

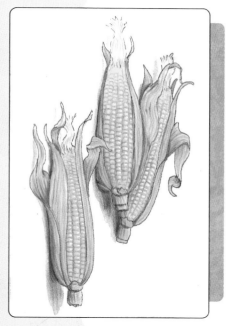

Many Aboriginal peoples all over North America grew corn. After they harvested the cobs, they dried them in the sun and then stored them in pits they dug into the ground. When the pits were full, they covered them up with a layer of grass, then a layer of soil, and then a layer of ashes.

Sometimes the corn was pounded into a powder on rocks or in wooden bowls. Afterward, the powdered corn, called cornmeal, was used to make a kind of porridge, and tortillas, and fried bread.

By drying corn and making cornmeal, Aboriginal peoples had corn available for them to eat all winter long.

What Did You Learn?

1. Of all the different uses for plants, which use do you think is the most important? Why?

2. Which use for plants were you most surprised to learn about? What surprised you?

3. What type of plant food is your favourite? What type of plant food do you like the least?

4. List some different ways you can eat your mystery food.

INVESTIGATING FURTHER

Processed Plants

Explain how one plant is changed as it is made into a food. Use drawings to show each step.

PLANTS IN GROUPS

Some plants are important foods. Some plants are not foods. Some plants are poisonous.

To help study plants, scientists sort them into groups. In Getting Started you will sort pictures of plants into groups. In Let's Observe you will sort plants that grow in your community. In Investigating Further you can learn how the plants in a supermarket are sorted.

GETTING STARTED

Look at the plants in this picture. How are they the same? How are they different? In a small group, decide on a way to sort the plants into groups. Be sure to explain why you grouped the plants the way you did. Compare how you sorted the plants with the way other groups in your class sorted their plants.

LET'S OBSERVE

Take a walk on the wild side. Look at the plants in your neighbourhood and see how many different ways you can sort them.

1. Take a walk and look at the plants you see.

2. In your science journal, write what each plant looks like, smells like, and feels like. You can look for some of these things:
   - Where is the plant growing?
   - Who planted it? How can you tell?
   - How big is it?
   - What colour is it?
   - What other plants does it look like?
   - What do people use it for?

3. In your science journal, draw each plant you see.

4. After you have looked at many plants, sort them into groups.

1. How did you choose groups for the plants?
2. What else would you like to learn about the plants you saw?

SCIENTISTS IN ACTION

Classifying Plants

Scientists are very serious about sorting or grouping plants. They call it classifying. Classifying plants helps them to know exactly which plant they are studying and what other plants it is similar to.

Scientists look for things that are the same when they classify plants. They look for ways that plants grow that are the same. Scientists have put the plants in this picture into the same group.

peach   cherry   plum

What Did You Learn?

1. What did you learn about the plants in your neighbourhood?
2. How can looking carefully help you classify plants?
3. What other things do you classify in everyday life?

INVESTIGATING FURTHER

Groups in the Supermarket

Supermarkets group their plant foods in a certain way. The next time you are in a supermarket, look carefully to see how they sort their plant foods. Find out why they group their plant foods the way they do.

GOING TO SEED

Many plants grow from seeds. We can eat some seeds, too. What kinds of seeds do you eat? What would happen if you planted those seeds?

In Getting Started you will match some seeds to the plant they come from. In Let's Investigate you will observe some seeds as they sprout. In Investigating Further you can take a closer look at the seeds you find on the ground.

1

2

3

4

5

6

7

8

9

10

11

GETTING STARTED

Play a matching game. Look at the pictures of seeds on page 38. Match as many as you can to the plant they come from on this page.

LET'S INVESTIGATE

How does a seed sprout? Take a closer look at sprouting seeds.

You will need
- bean seeds
- water
- a magnifier
- modelling clay
- a small paper plate or margarine lid
- a toothpick
- a plastic cup
- a knife

1. Soak the seeds overnight in water.
2. Cut one seed in half. Look at it carefully. Describe it in your science journal.
3. Put a small piece of modelling clay on a plate or lid.
4. Press a bean onto the sharp end of a toothpick. Stand the toothpick up in the modelling clay.
5. Place the plastic cup over top of the seed and set it near a window, but not in the sun.
6. Predict what you think will happen to the seed.
7. Sprinkle a few drops of water on your seed every day.
8. Describe how your seed changes in your science journal.
9. After your investigation is over, cut the seed in half and examine it. Compare it to your sketch of the first seed you cut in half.

Reflect on Your Results

1. How accurate was your prediction?

2. How did you help the seed sprout?

A sketch is a great way to record your observations.

INFORMATION STATION

The Beginning

Every seed contains the beginning of a new plant and some food for that plant. When a plant first starts to grow, it gets its energy from the food stored in the seed.

When a young shoot or stem breaks out of the seed's coat and starts to grow, we say the seed germinates.

A seed needs water, air, and warmth to germinate. Some seeds need light, too. When you water a seed, something inside the seed signals it to start growing. Until the stem grows leaves, the food stored inside the seed gives the new plant energy to grow.

Not all plants start from seeds. Some start from bulbs and some start from stems.

▲ These tulips grew from bulbs.

▲ Strawberry plants send out long runners. New plants will grow at the ends of the runners.

For a story about how one girl finds new life in a few seeds, look for this book: **A Handful of Seeds** by Monica Hughes (Lester Publishing: Toronto, ON, 1993).

SCIENCE IN OUR LIVES

Growing Vegetables

When you grow your own vegetables, you can watch the little seeds turn into delicious food. All you need is some soil, some water, and the seeds.

When you grow food from seeds, you will get better results if you follow these tips. (Check the package your seeds came in to see what your seeds need.)

1. Plant your garden at the right time. If you plant too early, the tiny plants might die in the cold weather. If you plant too late, the food might not have time to ripen before it gets cold in the fall.

radish   lettuce   carrot   bush bean   pepper   tomato   pole bean

2. Some plants will grow taller than others. Arrange your garden so that the taller plants don't block the sun from the shorter plants.

3. Plants need room to grow. Plant vegetables so that each type has enough room to grow.

4. Plant your seeds in neat rows. Then you will be able to tell the weeds from the food plants.

5. Pick the weeds as they start to grow. Any plant that isn't growing in a row is probably a weed.

What Did You Learn?

1. Draw a series of pictures to show what happens when a seed sprouts.

2. If a younger child asked you how plants started to grow, what would you say?

INVESTIGATING FURTHER

Wandering Seeds

Some seeds travel a great distance before they begin to sprout. Some, like dandelion seeds, float through the air. Others travel in different ways.

Take a sock walk. Wear an old sock over one shoe and walk through a park. Take off the sock and look at what seeds have stuck to your sock. Plant the seeds and see if they grow.

ROOTING FOR ROOTS

Have you ever heard someone say, "My roots are in the country"? What do you think they mean? What does this have to do with plants?

When a plant starts to grow up, it also starts to grow down. We call the down side of a plant its roots. Some of the vegetables we eat are actually roots. What roots do you like to eat?

In **Getting Started** you will ask others about their favourite root foods. In **Let's Observe** you will look closely at some growing roots. In **Investigating Further** you can learn when soil becomes important to a plant.

GETTING STARTED

Carrots, beets, radishes, horseradishes, ginger, and tapioca are all roots. Make a list of roots you like to eat. What do they all have in common? What's different about each one? Then ask 10 people what their favourite root foods are. Draw a pictograph to show people's favourite root foods.

Read the Toolkit on page 243 to see how to make a pictograph.

LET'S OBSERVE

A plant's roots sometimes seem to be growing in all directions. Grow some roots and watch what happens.

1. Soak the beans in the jar of water overnight.

2. Empty the jar. Crumple up one or two paper towels and place them in the jar.

3. Place the four seeds between the towel and the glass. Place one seed so it is pointing up, another so it's pointing down, the third pointing left, and the last one pointing right.

4. Pour some water into the jar to make the towel wet. Make sure the water doesn't cover the seeds. Put the lid on the jar.

5. Predict what will happen to the beans. Write your predictions in your journal.

6. Check the towel every day to see that it is moist, but that the beans are not sitting in water. Sprinkle some water on the towel if it is dry.

7. After about a week, turn the jar upside down.

You will need
- 4 bean seeds
- a glass jar with lid
- water
- paper towels

Reflect on Your Results

1. What happened to the bean seeds?

2. How were the roots that grew from each bean seed similar? How were they different?

3. What happened when you turned the jar upside down?

4. What do you think will happen if you let the bean seeds grow some more?

INFORMATION STATION

Root Work

A root has two important jobs. It keeps the plant from falling over and it brings minerals and water to the plant so the plant can grow. There are two kinds of roots that do this job.

A tap root is one long, thick root like a carrot. Dandelions have tap roots. They reach far down into the soil to get water for the plant even when the surface of the soil is very dry.

A fibrous root branches into many smaller roots. It can gather water and other things the plant needs from a wide area. Trees have fibrous roots.

What Did You Learn?

1. How can the shape of a root help it get water?
2. Some trees have roots as tall as the tree. Why do you think these plants have roots that long?
3. Why do you think the roots of your bean seeds grew in the direction they did?

INVESTIGATING FURTHER

When Do Plants Need Soil?

Your bean seeds began to grow roots without any soil. When will the tiny bean plants begin to need soil?

Plan an experiment to find out when bean plants begin to need soil. Tell your teacher what you plan to do. Gather the materials you need, and do your experiment. Describe everything you do and everything that happens in your science journal.

Tell the class what you learned.

SURPRISING STEMS

A stem is the part of the plant that connects its leaves to its roots. Stems come in many shapes and sizes. Look at the stems in this picture. What do you find surprising?

In **Getting Started** you will investigate how a drinking straw works and talk about how it is like a plant stem. In **Let's Investigate** you will see a colourful way of watching a stem in action. In **Investigating Further** you can experiment to find out how fast a stem grows.

GETTING STARTED

Make a list of all the stems you eat. Which one is your favourite? Which one is your least favourite?

Place a drinking straw in a glass of water. Blow gently. What happens? What happens when you suck in? How might this be similar to a plant stem?

LET'S INVESTIGATE

Watch some stems in action! This investigation has some colourful results.

1. Cut off the bottom end of the celery. Leave the leafy part on top.

2. Add two or three drops of blue or red food colouring to a jar of water. Stir it to mix in the food colouring.

3. Place the celery in the jar of water.

You will need
- a stalk of celery
- glass jars
- blue or red food colouring
- water
- a spoon
- a knife
- a magnifier

Handle the knife carefully.

You can do the same experiment with a white carnation.

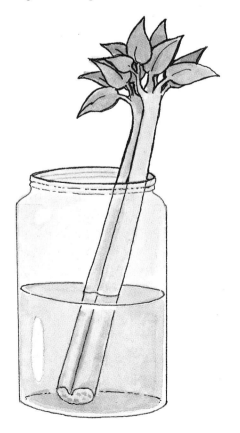

4. Observe the celery every couple of hours. Describe what you see in your science journal.

5. After a day, remove the celery from the jar. Cut a piece off the bottom end of the celery about 2 cm long.

6. Observe the piece of celery with your magnifier. What do you see?

Reflect on Your Results

1. What does the food colouring help you to see?

2. What does the piece of celery have in common with the straw you sucked on earlier?

INFORMATION STATION

Inside a Stem

The stem is the part of the plant that holds it up above ground. The leaves of the plant need sunlight, and the stem holds them up where they can get it.

The roots of a plant get water from the soil. Tubes run up and down the inside of the stem, carrying water to the leaves and carrying food down to be stored in the roots.

Sap is a watery liquid made by the leaves that travels through the stem's tubes to feed the plant. The milky substance that comes out of a dandelion stem when you pick it is a type of sap.

Some plant stems are very thin and flexible. Think of a vine plant like peas or ivy.

Other stems are very thick and strong. Think of the biggest tree you've ever seen.

The bark on a tree is the outer coating of its stem. It protects the tree. That's why it's important to never peel the bark off a tree. Each type of tree has its own bark pattern.

Syrupy Sap

The sap from some kinds of trees is sweet. Sugar maple trees are tapped for their syrup. In the spring, when the sap stored in the roots begins to flow up through the stem to the branches so new leaves can grow, a small hole is drilled into the tree trunk. Then a bucket is attached to the tree so that a small amount of the sap will drip into the bucket. After the sap is collected, it is boiled down and made into maple syrup. Yum!

Sometimes the sap is collected in long tubes that go from tree to tree. Then no one has to travel from tree to tree emptying buckets.

You might enjoy reading about a grandfather who teaches his grandson how to make maple sugar. Look for this book: ***At Grandpa's Sugar Bush*** by Margaret Carney (Kids Can Press: Toronto, ON, 1997).

What Did You Learn?

1. What is the same about all plant stems? What can be different?
2. What ways do you use plant stems at home? at school?
3. What are a stem's most important jobs?

INVESTIGATING FURTHER

Measuring Stem Growth

How quickly does a stem grow? Design an experiment using bean seeds in soil to find out how quickly a bean plant stem grows compared to the roots or the leaves.

FOOD FACTORY

Plants are different from other living things because they can make their own food. They make food in their leaves. There are only a few plants that catch food.

This pitcher plant is very unusual. It uses its leaves to catch insects for dinner.

In Getting Started you will sort plants by their leaves. In Let's Investigate you will see how a plant depends on its leaves. In Investigating Further you can try growing new plants from leaves.

GETTING STARTED

Take a walk and collect some leaves. Choose leaves that have fallen to the ground or leaves from weeds. You can also collect some leaves from food plants. In a group, look at your leaves carefully. Use a magnifier. How are they similar? How are they different?

Sort the leaves into piles. How did you decide which pile to put a leaf in?

LET'S INVESTIGATE

What do leaves need to make food for plants?
Do this investigation to find out.

1. Cut a piece of aluminum foil about twice the size of one leaf on your plant.

2. Carefully cover both sides of one leaf with the foil.

3. Spread petroleum jelly on a second leaf. Make sure both the top and bottom of the leaf are covered.

4. Predict what will happen to both leaves. Write your predictions in your science journal.

5. Check the leaves on your plant daily. Describe what you see in your science journal.

You will need
- a healthy, leafy house plant
- aluminum foil
- petroleum jelly

Drawings are a good way to record what you see.

1. What happened to the leaf covered with aluminum foil? Why do you think this happened?

2. What happened to the leaf covered with petroleum jelly? Why do you think this happened?

INFORMATION STATION

Inside a Leaf

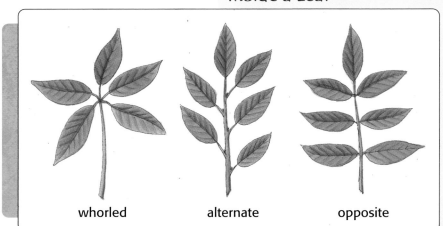

whorled   alternate   opposite

A leaf is the food factory of a plant. During the day it takes in energy from the sun and carbon dioxide from the air and water from the soil. The leaf uses these things to make food. The leaf also makes small amounts of oxygen and water.

Leaves are usually very flat. This helps the leaf get as much sun as possible. It also helps get carbon dioxide and oxygen from the air to all parts of the leaf.

Leaves come in many shapes. You can often tell what kind of plant a leaf is from by looking at its shape. Look at the leaves you collected. Decide what plants some of them came from.

Leaves are also sorted by how they grow on the stem. Three different ways are shown in the picture above.

Most evergreen trees have leaves that are so thin they don't even look like leaves. We call them needles. Evergreen needles have a coating of wax to keep them from drying out. This makes evergreen trees with needles well suited to growing in dry places.

Maple trees are famous for their colours in the autumn.

What Did You Learn?

1. What might happen to the leaves of a plant if it was not watered?

2. What do leaves need to make food for plants?

3. Why is it important to observe carefully and to record what you observe?

INVESTIGATING FURTHER

Planting Leaves

Sometimes a new plant can be grown from just one leaf. Try it out. Cut a leaf off a houseplant such as an African violet. Put the leaf on some soil. Keep the soil moist. Check your leaf every few days to see what happens.

FLOWERS AND FRUITS

The prettiest part of a plant is its flower. The fruit is delicious to eat. But flowers and fruits aren't just to look at or to taste. They play an important part in the life of a plant.

In Getting Started you will talk about the flowers that you know. In Let's Observe you will take a closer look at a flower and a fruit. In Investigating Further you can learn how colour is important to plants.

GETTING STARTED

Take a walk in your neighbourhood. Make notes and sketches of the flowers you see. If it isn't flower-blooming time, then brainstorm a list of flowers you know that grow where you live. Compare your list with the flowers on page 58.

LET'S OBSERVE

To find out how important flowers and fruits are to the life of a plant, make some close observations.

PART 1: A CLOSER LOOK AT A FLOWER

1. Look carefully at your flower. Smell it. Notice its colour and all its parts. Use the magnifier to look at it.

2. Draw your flower in your science journal. Label your drawing.

3. Look at the petals. How many are there? How are they attached to the flower? Where might an insect land on this flower?

4. Carefully remove the petals from your flower.

5. There should be several thin stalks in the centre of the flower. These are called the stamens. Touch the end of one of the stamens with your finger. The powder that comes off is called pollen. What colour is it?

6. In the middle of the stamens should be one stalk with a bulge at the bottom of it. This is called the pistil.

You will need
- one of these flowers: petunia, snapdragon, tulip, daffodil, morning glory
- a ruler
- a magnifier
- a knife

Knives are sharp.

7. Carefully cut the bulge in half with a knife. Using your magnifier, look for seeds inside it.

8. Describe or sketch everything you notice in your science journal.

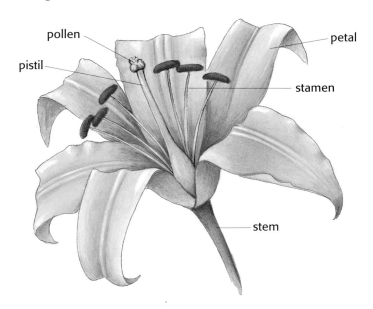

If you want to read more about flowers, look for this book:
Flowers
by David Burnie
(Stoddart: Toronto, ON, 1992).

You will need
- one of these fruits: apple, squash, orange, grape, cucumber
- a magnifier
- a knife
- paper towels
- an aluminum pie plate
- poster paints
- white paper

Reflect on Your Results

1. Which parts were you able to identify on your flower?

2. What did you see when you looked at the inside of the bulge at the bottom of the pistil?

3. How did a magnifier help you to observe your flower carefully?

PART 2: A CLOSER LOOK AT A FRUIT

1. Carefully examine your fruit. Notice its colour and all of its parts. Smell it. Use a magnifier to look at it more closely.

2. Describe or sketch what you see in your science journal.

3. Cut your fruit in half. Where are the seeds? How many are there?

4. Compare your fruit with that of another classmate. How are they the same? How are they different?

5. Cover the bottom of a pie plate with poster paint.

6. Dip the cut side of your piece of fruit into the paint. Be sure the fruit is evenly covered with paint.

7. Press your fruit onto white paper. Press carefully so the fruit doesn't move.

8. Lift the fruit to see your fruit print.

9. Try different fruits and colours to make an attractive design.

If your fruit is hard, ask an adult to help you cut it.

If you use large sheets of newsprint, you can make some interesting gift wrap with your fruit prints.

Reflect on Your Results

1. How were the fruits the same? How were they different?

2. How were the seeds in your fruit similar to the seeds in another fruit? How were they different?

Busy as a Bee

A bee collects nectar from thousands of flowers to make a small amount of honey.

When bees collect nectar, they also collect pollen on their legs and bodies. They leave some of this pollen on other flowers they visit. Some of the pollen rubs off on the pistils of the flowers, and that's when seeds and fruit start growing. Farmers love having bees around because they help fruit grow.

Other insects visit flowers and move pollen around, too. Some pollen is carried by the wind.

Once the fruit grows and ripens, birds and animals eat it. When a bird or another animal eats fruit, they may leave the seeds far from the plant the fruit came from. This helps the plant spread its seeds around. How do other seeds travel?

What Did You Learn?

1. How do bees help a plant when they collect nectar from the plant?

2. How do animals help a plant when they eat its fruit?

INVESTIGATING FURTHER

Fruity Ink

Flowers and fruits come in many beautiful colours. Find out why colours are so important to the life of a plant. Then make some berry ink to see how the colour of fruit can be used in a practical way. First, mash some blueberries or strawberries with a spoon. Add a little water. Then strain your berry mash through a layer of paper towel spread over a small jar. When all the liquid has drained through the towel, throw away the towel and the remains of the berries. The liquid in the jar is your ink. You can cut one end of a drinking straw on an angle and use it to write with your ink.

FROM SEED TO SEED

In this unit you have learned how each part of a plant helps the plant grow. Now it's time to put it all together!

In Getting Started you will put the life cycle of a flower in its proper order. In Let's Observe you will collect parts of a plant and use them to show the life cycle of a plant. In Investigating Further you can learn why leaves turn colour in the fall.

GETTING STARTED

These pictures show the life cycle of a poppy flower. With a partner, write the numbers in the proper order in your science journal. Start with seeds.

LET'S OBSERVE

Scientists like to collect things. It helps them learn more about them. Collect your own parts of a plant to help you learn about the life cycle of the plant.

1. Collect flowers, seeds, nuts or fruit, and leaves from one kind of plant. If you can't collect some of these, gather pictures of plants from magazines.

2. Press the leaves and flowers to preserve them. You can use a plant press to do this, or you can place them between paper towels underneath a stack of heavy books for several days. You can dry small fruits on a windowsill in the sun.

You will need
- leaves
- flowers
- seeds
- magazine pictures of plants
- a plant press or paper towels and heavy books
- materials for a display

Be sure to ask permission before picking any part of a growing plant.

3. Decide how to display your collection. You can display it in a scrapbook, on a display table, or on poster board.

- Arrange your plant parts to show the life cycle of a plant. Show each stage of its life.
- Label each stage. Label the time of year each stage occurs. For example, a tulip bulb is planted in the fall and the flower blooms in the spring.

Reflect on Your Results

1. What are the main stages that the plant you collected goes through in a year?

2. What new questions do you have after displaying the life of your plant?

For a fun look at the life cycle of a watermelon, look for this book:
A Seed Grows
by Pamela Hickman
(Kids Can Press: Toronto, ON, 1997).

What Did You Learn?

1. What did you learn about the plant you collected that you didn't know before?

2. How do the seasons affect the life cycle of plants?

3. Why do scientists who study plants need to pay attention to the seasons?

INVESTIGATING FURTHER

Look in the Toolkit on page 244 to learn about gathering information from library books.

Colourful Leaves

A flower is colourful as it blooms, but leaves turn colour after they die. Find out why.

Thinking About Growing Green

1. Which of these two stems would support the largest plant? Why?

2. What is your favourite plant? Draw a picture of it. Explain what you like about it.

3. Answer this riddle. The answer is a part of a plant.

> I use sunlight and water to make food.
> What am I?

4. Make up a riddle about another part of a plant.

5. List three ways that people use plants.

6. List three ways that people can help plants.

7. How does looking very carefully help you learn about plants?

The Builders

Wherever we go, we see structures. People have built some of them. Animals are good designers and builders too.

A structure is something that has been built and has a purpose, or a job. Look at the structures in the picture.

- Who built them?
- What jobs do they do?
- How have materials been joined together to make them?

In this unit you will design and build structures. Tools make it easier to build things. So you will learn how to choose tools and use them safely. Like a scientist, you will also test the building materials you use and your structures themselves.

Tower Power

Towers come in different sizes and shapes. They are made using all sorts of materials. All towers must be strong and stable. If they aren't, they may fall over.

In what ways are the towers in the photos the same? different? What makes them strong?

In Getting Started you will use your body to find out what makes a tower stable. In Let's Investigate you will build two different towers and compare their strength. In Investigating Further you can talk about the strength of different thicknesses of plywood.

GETTING STARTED

Which student in this picture would be the most difficult to push off balance? Why? Write your prediction in your science journal.

Work with three other classmates. Take turns standing or lying down like each of the children in the picture. Try pushing each person off balance. Use the same amount of push, or force, each time.

Which position can you knock someone off balance from most easily? Which is the hardest to push someone off balance from? Why? Which position is the most stable?

Stop pushing when your classmate begins to lose his or her balance. Don't make anyone fall.

You will need
- 30 old playing cards
- scissors
- a ruler or tape measure

A tower made of playing cards will fall down easily. Or will it? With a partner build two towers out of playing cards and compare their strength.

1. Use 12 playing cards to build a tower. Decide how to balance them to make them the most stable. Do not bend, fold, or cut the cards.

2. Estimate the height of your tower. Use a tape measure or ruler to measure it. Write the height you thought it might be and its real height in your science journal.

3. Brainstorm ways that folding or cutting the cards might make them into better building blocks. Try folding and cutting a few cards and building with them.

4. Use 12 playing cards to build a second tower. This time, use some of your ideas from step 3 to make your tower stronger.

5. Estimate the height of your tower. Then, check your estimate by measuring your tower. Write down your estimate and measurement.

6. Plan how you could compare the strength of your two towers. Then, test the towers.

Comparing Towers			
Tower	Estimated height	Measured height	Strength
1			
2			

◄Using a chart like this to record your estimates and measurements can help you to keep track of them.

Reflect on Your Results

1. Which tower was stronger? How could you tell?

2. Why do you think one tower was stronger than the other?

3. How could you make the stronger tower even stronger?

Strong, Stable Structures

Towers, bridges, honeycombs, and eggshells are just a few of the many kinds of structures in the world.

A structure has to stand up to forces that may push on it. A force is a push, pull, or twist that can make an object move or change direction.

You made a structure when you built a tower out of playing cards. If you tested its strength by blowing on it, then you applied a force to your structure.

The second tower you made probably didn't wobble as much as the first one. The second tower was more stable.

In some parts of the world, buildings must stand up to strong winds or earthquakes. In other places, they have to stand under lots of rain or heavy snow.

What forces are being applied to the structures shown in this picture? Which structures do you think can stand up best to these forces? Why?

What Did You Learn?

1. How could you make the card towers you built stronger? Explain why you would make each change.

2. List five forces a structure might have to stand up to.

3. Look at the structures in the Information Station. Some were made by animals and others by humans. Which are stronger? What is different about the materials that animals use to build structures and those that humans use?

INVESTIGATING FURTHER

Stacked for Strength

Much of the world's plywood is made in Canada. Plywood is made up of sheets of wood held together with strong glue. It comes in different thicknesses.

Why do you think plywood comes in different thicknesses?

Talk with a partner about what parts of a house you might need to use thick plywood for. Why? What parts could you use thin plywood for? Why?

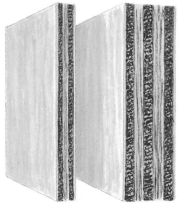

▲ thin plywood   ▲ thick plywood

Mighty Materials

The materials you choose when you build a structure are important. The stronger your materials, the stronger your structure will be.

In **Getting Started** you will compare three different structures. In **Let's Experiment** you will test two materials to find out which is stronger. In **Investigating Further** you can create an advertisement for a great building material.

Read the definition of a structure on page 69.

GETTING STARTED

Work with a partner. Which of the objects in the picture is a structure? Explain why each is or isn't a structure.

Choose three structures from the picture on page 76. Make sure at least one structure was made by an animal.

What is the same about the structures you chose? What is different? Which structure do you think is the strongest? Which is the most stable? Can any be unsafe? Can any harm the environment? Which are well made? Give reasons for all your answers.

INFORMATION STATION

Fair Tests

Scientists use something called a fair test to make sure they get useful results. This means they make sure everything in the test, or experiment, stays the same—except the thing being tested.

For example, suppose a scientist wanted to test the strength of two types of sticky tape. She would keep the amount of tape and the surface the tape sticks on the same. In each test, she would only change the type of tape used.

Scientists call something that can be changed a variable. These are some of the variables in the sticky-tape test:

- the amount of tape
- the surface the tape sticks on
- the type of tape used

In a fair test, you only change the variable you want to test.

What if the scientist who tested the sticky tape didn't conduct a fair test? Then, we couldn't be sure the tape was as strong or as sticky as the test showed. When tests are fair, we know that the results are accurate.

When you are testing something, make a chart of the variables. Decide which variable you need to change and which ones you need to keep the same.

A Fair Test	
The one thing I will change	The things I will keep the same
• type of tape	• amount of tape I use • surface on which I stick the tape • other variables

You will need
- 2 types of glue
- 2 types of string or thread
- 2 types of drinking straws
- 2 types of sticky tape
- craft sticks

Sometimes we need materials to be strong so that they can hold up heavy loads. Other times we need flexible materials that can bend and then come back to their original shape and size.

In a small group, test some building materials to see what you might use them for.

1. Design a fair test to answer one of these questions:
   - Which type of string is stronger?
   - Which type of drinking straw is more flexible?
   - Which tape sticks better?
   - Which glue works better?

2. Make a chart of your variables like the one in the Information Station on page 77. Put this in your science journal.

3. Design a fair test for any other question you might have about the materials you have gathered.

4. Conduct your tests. Record your results.

Reflect on Your Results

1. How did you make sure your test was fair?

2. What forces—pushes, pulls, or twists—did each material you tested have to stand up to?

3. If another group tested the same materials yours did, compare your results with theirs. How were their results similar to yours? different?

To find out more about materials that animals use to build structures, look for *Animal Homes* by Barbara Taylor (Firefly Books: Willowdale, ON, 1996).

What Did You Learn?

1. Why is it important to conduct fair tests on materials?

2. Which of the materials you tested would you use to build a tower? Why?

INVESTIGATING FURTHER

Tests Show...

Design an advertisement for one of the materials you tested. Tell people why the material is a good one. Also, give them ideas about how they might use the material. Use your fair-test results to help you do this. Include a picture of the material doing its job.

Tests show it even holds up lunch boxes!

Tool Talk

All builders use tools. Tools allow us to do certain jobs or help us do them better. Which tools have you seen or used before? What jobs do they help people do?

In **Getting Started** you will talk about tools. In **Let's Investigate** you will use tools to build a small structure. In **Investigating Further** you can use your tool skills to make a picture frame.

GETTING STARTED

Look at the tools in the picture on page 80. With a partner, name the ones you recognize. Which tools are new to you? What do you think these might be used for?

What safety rules should you follow when you use any of these tools? Why are safety rules important?

LET'S INVESTIGATE

Work with a partner to build a structure using tools.

1. Use a saw and mitre box to cut a piece of wood 10 cm long. Remember to put on your safety goggles before you start. How can you tell that the wood is exactly 10 cm long?

2. Repeat step 1 with three other pieces of wood.

3. Cut a triangle out of cardboard with some scissors. The triangle must have a right angle like the one in the picture. Make two sides of the triangle 3 cm long.

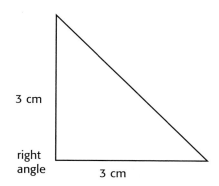

You will need
- a saw
- a mitre box
- pieces of wood about 2 cm x 2 cm x 15 cm
- safety goggles
- a tape measure
- scissors
- cardboard
- glue

Be very careful when cutting with a saw. Ask your teacher to show you how to use a mitre box safely.

4. Repeat step 3 to make three more triangles.

5. Use glue and your cardboard triangles to join the 4 pieces of wood together in a square like the one in the picture.

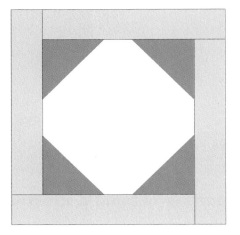

6. Use any tools, pieces of wood, glue, and as many right-angled triangles as you need to make a chair, a table, or another structure. You can use the square you have already built as part of this structure.

7. Compare your structure with one made by another pair of students. With the other pair of students, design and conduct a fair test to find out which structure is stronger.

Reflect on Your Results

1. How did tools help you build your square?

2. How did the triangles help you build the square? What would happen to your square if you didn't use the triangles?

3. What job does your final structure do?

The Right Tool for the Job

John Thorneloe works as a carpenter and construction foreman in Sydney, British Columbia. He builds houses and apartment buildings. As a hobby, he likes to make furniture and boats.

What skills and interests do you need to be a carpenter?
You have to like hard work, enjoy carpentry (working with wood), and have special skills such as knowing how to read building plans.

How long did it take to become a carpenter?
I worked in construction jobs for about 10 years. Then I did my training, which is called an apprenticeship. That took four years. During that time, I went to carpentry school for six weeks each year and worked at my construction job for the rest of the year.

The students have been working with cutting tools. What building materials do you have to cut?
We cut concrete, wood, steel, and drywall. When we cut concrete, we might use a jackhammer or sledgehammer. When we cut wood, we use anything from a handsaw, a chisel, or a knife right up to the most expensive table saws, radial-arm saws, and power mitre saws. The students might know about a mitre box. A mitre saw does the same job, but it's motorized and much faster.

What safety equipment do you use when you're working?
When I use my power tools, I wear hearing protection and special safety goggles. At any construction site, we must wear hard hats and steel-toed boots.

How do you care for your tools?
I keep them clean and dry. Keeping tools dry is very hard to do when I'm working outside framing a house in southern British Columbia. Also, I always make sure my saws have sharp edges. A sharp edge is less dangerous than a dull edge.

What Did You Learn?

1. What tools did you use to build your structure?

2. Which of the tools described in Scientists in Action might have helped you when you were building your structure?

3. Why are safety rules important to follow?

4. Draw a diagram of the structure you made, and use arrows to show where you put forces when you tested it.

INVESTIGATING FURTHER

Frame Yourself

Picture frames often have a square or rectangular shape. Look closely at the picture frames in your home. What shapes do they have? What materials are they made of? How have the parts been joined together? Make some notes about how they are made in your science journal.

Use materials and tools at home to make a picture frame. Show your picture frame to the class. Discuss how you could make it stronger.

Lever Lift

A lever is a tool used for moving things, often for lifting things. Find the levers in the picture below. What jobs do they do? What do these levers have in common?

In Getting Started you will use a lever to solve a problem. In Let's Investigate you will look at how levers work and then design your own lever. In Investigating Further you can play a lever game.

GETTING STARTED

The only tool you have is a spoon. How can you open a tin of cocoa with it? Work with a partner, and find a way to solve the problem.

Once you have the tin open, close it again. Try to open it without the spoon. How does using the spoon make it easier to open the tin?

LET'S INVESTIGATE

Explore how levers work, and find a way to make lifting things easier. Then, design you own lever.

PART ONE

You will need
- 3 pencils
- sticky tape
- a ruler
- 5 pennies

1. Tape three pencils together in a bundle with two on the bottom and one on top. Then, tape the bundle to a desk so that the pencils stay in one place.

2. Place a ruler on the pencils so that the pencils are exactly in the middle of the ruler. The ruler should balance on the pencils.

3. Stack two pennies together. Put them on the ruler 3 cm from the pencils. What happens? Why?

4. Repeat step 3, but tape the pennies on to the ruler. Put another penny on the ruler on the other side of the pencils. Place this penny 3 cm from the pencils as well. What happens? Why?

5. Move the single penny slowly away from the pencils. How far do you have to move it before the ruler balances?

Think about your own experiences on a seesaw.

6. Record your results in your science journal using a chart like this one.

Lifting a Load With a Lever	
Number of pennies 3 cm from the pencils	Where I put the single penny so that the ruler balanced
2	? cm from the pencils
3	
4	

7. Try the same test with three pennies taped to the ruler. Then, try it with four pennies. Record where you have to put the single penny to balance the ruler each time.

Reflect on Your Results

1. How did you use a single penny to lift two, three, and four pennies?

2. How could you use what you learned to help you lift a heavy toy box onto a table by yourself?

3. Explain what you did to be sure each test was fair.

PART TWO

You will need
- 3 thumb tacks
- 3 strips of thin cardboard 15 cm x 2 cm
- thick cardboard from a box

Tacks are sharp. Use them carefully. Keep them in a safe container.

1. Press a thumb tack through the middle of one of the thin strips of cardboard and into a thick piece of cardboard.

2. Push the strip so that it turns to the right around the thumb tack. You've made a lever!

3. Press a thumb tack through the bottom end of another thin strip and into the thick cardboard.

4 Push this strip so that it turns to the right around its thumb tack. In your science journal, describe how it moves differently than your first strip did.

5. Press a thumb tack through the top end of the third strip and into the thick cardboard.

6. Push this strip so that it turns to the right around its thumb tack. Record how it moves differently than your first or second lever did.

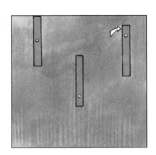

7. Use what you now know about levers to design a building tool. You don't have to make the tool. Just draw a picture of it in your science journal.

Sketch ideas for your lever design on scrap paper. Then, draw the final design in your science journal.

Reflect on Your Results

1. How is the lever you designed similar to the levers construction workers use? How is it different?

INFORMATION STATION

Levers Work All Around Us

A lever may be a simple tool, but it does an important job. It can help you put more force on an object that is difficult to move. A lever can turn a small movement at one end of it into a larger one at the other.

The point on which a lever balances or turns is called the fulcrum. All levers have fulcrums. The force applied to a lever is called the effort. This effort can be a push, a pull, or a twist. The object that the lever moves is called the load.

You can use a lever to open a cocoa tin. When you put one end of the spoon under the lid and push down on the other end, the spoon acts as a lever. The edge of the tin is the fulcrum. The lid of the tin is the load you move, and your hand provides the effort.

A lever makes the job of moving something easier. This is because it can change a small force into a bigger force. You saw this when you lifted two, three, and then four pennies using a single penny's worth of effort.

We use levers when we cut with scissors or dig with a shovel. We use special levers as tools to build structures.

To help you remember what science words mean, write their meanings in your own words. Add pictures if that helps to make the meanings clearer.

What Did You Learn?

1. Circle the fulcrum of the lever tool you designed.

2. Explain to a classmate how a lever works. Use the words you learned in the Information Station. You can use your cardboard levers to help you explain.

3. How could you balance on a seesaw with someone who weighs more than you?

INVESTIGATING FURTHER

To find out more about levers, look for **Lifting by Levers** by Andrew Dunn (Wayland Publishers: New York, U.S., 1993).

Spot the Lever

Find levers in your classroom, around the school, and at home. Explain why each object is a lever. How does each one help people do a job? Make a class list of levers. How many did your class find?

Stable Shapes

Towers serve many different purposes. This makes them fun to build and interesting to look at. Some towers are shaped a certain way to give them extra support.

In Getting Started you will talk about tower shapes. In Let's Experiment you will build three different towers and test their strength. In Investigating Further you can research a tower that interests you.

GETTING STARTED

What do you think each tower in the picture on page 91 is used for? How are the towers similar? different? What shapes do you see in the towers? How might these shapes make the towers stronger? Discuss these questions as a class.

LET'S EXPERIMENT

You will need
- drinking straws
- a roll of string
- 4 paper clips
- measuring tape
- loads to test the towers
- sticky tape
- a balance or scale (optional)

How can you give a tower extra support? Build three different towers to find out.

1. Work in a small group. Use 20 drinking straws and string to build Tower 1. Make it look like the one in this picture.

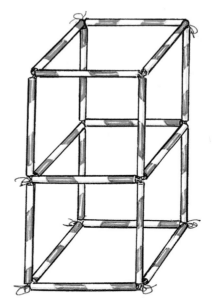

2. Design a test to determine the strength of your tower. Think about how you could slowly put more weight on it.

3. Make a chart like this one in your science journal to record your results.

Comparing Tower Strength			
	Tower 1	Tower 2	Tower 3
test 1	stood up to 240 grams		
test 2			

You may want to use a balance or scale to find out exactly how much weight you put on your tower.

4. Conduct your test.

5. Build Tower 2. Start by making a tower exactly like Tower 1. Add more drinking straws crossing from corner to corner of each square panel. The picture below shows some finished panels.

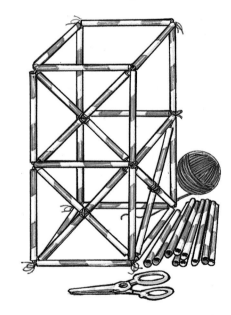

6. Test the strength of Tower 2 using the same tests you designed for Tower 1. Make sure that you keep your tests fair. How do the test results compare with those for Tower 1?

7. Build Tower 3. Start by making a tower like Tower 1. Then,

- attach paper clips to the top four corners of the tower
- measure the height of the tower
- cut four pieces of string that are each 10 cm longer than that
- tie one piece of string to each paper clip
- tape the other end of each piece of string to your desk near the bottom of the tower

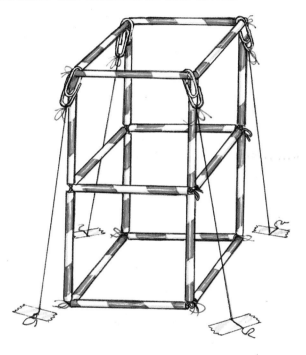

8. Test the strength of Tower 3. Do the same tests you used on Towers 1 and 2. Record your results.

Reflect on Your Results

To read about how to make a pictograph, look in the Toolkit on page 243.

1. Which tower was the strongest? the second strongest? the weakest? How can you tell?

2. Make a simple pictograph to show your test results. What does the graph tell you?

INFORMATION STATION

Simple Support

Structures have to stand up to different kinds of forces. They are built in different ways to do this.

Compression is a squeezing, or pushing, force. An example of compression is your hand squishing a milk carton.

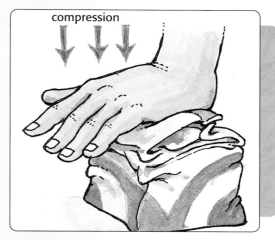

compression

Did you find that Tower 2 stood up to a weight placed on top of it better than Tower 1 or Tower 3 did? The drinking straws you crossed from corner to corner of the square panels in Tower 2 helped it resist the downward force of compression. We call a part of a structure that does this a strut.

Look closely at the struts in Tower 2. You'll see that they form triangles. Engineers often use triangles to build structures because the triangle is a very strong shape. It allows a structure to support heavy loads.

Another force that can act on a structure is a pulling force called tension.

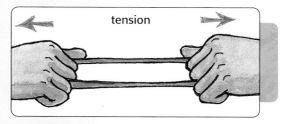

tension

If you tested your towers by pushing them from the side, did you find that Tower 3 was the hardest to push over? The strings you tied to the top corners of Tower 3 and taped down helped to keep it stable. When you pushed on the tower, tension pulled the strings tight. Strings or wires like these are called ties.

What other building shapes can you think of that help support a structure?

What Did You Learn?

1. Which of your towers would work best to hold up a heavy object. Why?

2. Which of your towers would be the most stable if a wind blew on it? Why?

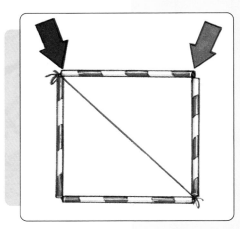

3. What would happen if you pushed the corner of the square in the picture where the red arrow is pointing? Record your prediction. Then test it. What happened? Why? Was it what you thought would happen?

4. What would happen if you pushed the corner where the blue arrow is pointing? Record your prediction. Then test it. What happened? Why? Was it what you thought would happen?

5. Which would be a stronger structure, a pyramid made of six drinking straws or a cube made of 12 drinking straws? Why?

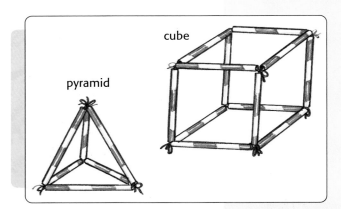

cube

pyramid

SCIENCE IN OUR LIVES

Waving Skyscrapers

Did you know that tall buildings can sway?

A building like the one in the picture can sway about a metre in any direction on very windy days. It must be built to stand up to forces caused by winds.

To help reduce swaying, some tall buildings have large weights on their roofs. These weights are on rollers attached to springs. When the wind makes the building sway one way, the weights move in the opposite direction. The force of the weights helps to balance out, or counterbalance, the force of the wind.

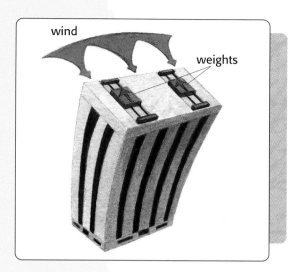

INVESTIGATING FURTHER

Learning More About Towers

Choose one of the types of towers in the picture on page 91 to research. Use these questions to help you:

- Where would I find one?
- What is the tower used for?
- What shape does the tower have?
- What materials were used to build it?

Share what you learn with the class. You may either make a display or give a presentation.

When you use a CD-ROM or the Internet, type in the name of the kind of building you want to search for information on.

Tower Design

Y**ou have so many things to think about when you build a tower. Seeing what you will do in a picture can make the job easier to understand. Plans help keep your ideas organized.**

In Getting Started you will look at and talk about a special kind of drawing. In Let's Explore you will work in a group to design and build a tower. In Investigating Further you can interview someone who designs or builds structures.

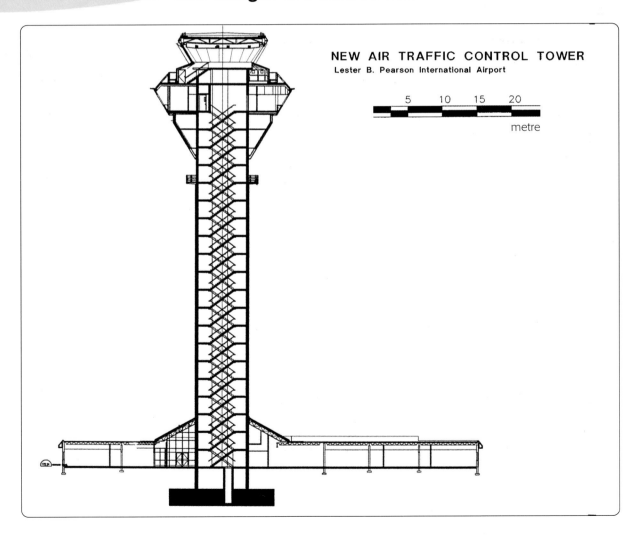

NEW AIR TRAFFIC CONTROL TOWER
Lester B. Pearson International Airport

5   10   15   20

metre

GETTING STARTED

What does the drawing on page 98 show? What information can you learn from it? How and why might the drawing be used?

When do you make plans? Why? Why might you write or draw them on paper?

LET'S EXPLORE

Ready for a challenge? You and a group of classmates will design and build a tower at least 50 cm high. It must have a platform that supports a load of at least 500 g.

1. Meet as a group to design your tower. Choose one person to be the recorder. This person will write down group ideas and decisions.

2. Brainstorm ideas for your tower. Also think about these planning questions:
   - What forces will affect our tower?
   - What shapes and features will we include in our tower to make it stronger?
   - What materials will we use?
   - How much of each material do we need?
   - How will we join these materials together?
   - What tools will we need?

3. Decide what needs to be done. Make a list of tasks. Decide who will do each task.

4. Test the strength of the materials you are thinking of using. Make sure your tests are fair. Record your test results in your science journal. Decide which of these materials will be strong enough to use for your tower.

You will need
- a large piece of unlined paper
- a ruler
- building materials you decide on

You may want to use a computer drawing program to make your final tower design.

5. Draw plans of what your tower will look like. Include labels for materials, measurements, and important tower features.

Look back over the notes in your science journal for this unit to find more ideas for your tower design.

6. Build your tower! If something in your design doesn't work, rethink your ideas. You will test your tower in the next learning event.

Reflect on Your Results

1. Which materials did you choose for your tower? Why?

2. Which shapes did you use in your tower design? Why?

3. What features of its design make your tower strong and stable?

Designing an Airport Tower

John Knox has been an architect for about 30 years. He has created many plans for airport buildings, including a new control tower at Pearson International Airport in Toronto. This is one of the largest airport control towers in Canada. It stands about 65 m tall and is made of about 4200 tonnes of concrete.

How long did it take to design and build the airport tower?

It took about two years of planning. Then a team spent a year and a half on the construction.

What is the purpose of the airport tower?

The air traffic controllers who work in the tower control all the flights coming in and going out of the airport. The control tower has to give clear lines of sight. That means the air traffic controllers must be able to see in all directions. They need a good view of all areas on the ground—the runways, taxiways, aprons, everything.

What steps did you go through when designing the tower?

We talked to the people who were going use the tower about what they wanted. From there we came up with our first design ideas. Then, we asked people about our ideas and produced a final design. Next, we made working—or technical—drawings, which contain lots of details.

Did you build models of the tower?

Yes. We built some rough models. We used them to solve design problems. Our client also built a detailed model that is very realistic. It even has flashing red airport lights. This model was used to show people what the completed tower would look like. ▶

▲ detailed model of the new control tower at Pearson International Airport

To find out more about building towers, look for ***Towers and Tunnels*** by Etta Kaner (Kids Can Press: Toronto, ON, 1995).

What forces did you have to think about when you designed the tower?

The main ones were wind and snow. The tower is designed to make sure it can stand up against wind. Most of the wind comes from the west. But wind can come from any side, so the tower had to be designed for wind forces from all sides. A circle is a very good shape for that.

What Did You Learn?

1. What new ideas about tower design did you learn from John Knox's interview?

2. Why do architects and engineers build models to test their design ideas? Why do they talk to the people who will use the structure?

INVESTIGATING FURTHER

Review the two interviews on page 83 and pages 101 and 102. Which questions gave good answers? Try using questions like these in your own interview.

Talking To Builders

There are many jobs in building design and construction. Some examples are architects and carpenters. Others include plumbers, electricians, drywallers, roofers, bricklayers, painters, floor layers, and cabinet installers.

Choose a building job that interests you. Interview someone who does that job. Take notes during the interview, or record the conversation. Share what you learn about the person's job with the class.

Testing Towers

Whenever you build something that will be used, it is a good idea to test it. Make sure it does what you built it to do. What is you tower built to do? How could you test your tower?

In Getting Started you will talk about why testing is so important. In Let's Observe you will use a checklist to judge your tower. In Investigating Further you can observe towers in your community and learn about one of them.

GETTING STARTED

The tower in the photo on page 103 is called the Leaning Tower of Pisa. This tower began to lean before the builders had even finished building it.

Talk with a partner about what might have gone wrong when this tower was built. What might the builders have tested before starting the tower? What do you think could be done to the tower now to keep it from leaning more?

LET'S OBSERVE

You will need
- your tower from Tower Design
- a measuring scale
- testing materials of your choice

Work with your tower-building group to test your tower platform and judge your tower's features.

1. Make a checklist in your science journal of features you will judge for your tower. You may want to include some of these features:
   - appearance (Does the design of your tower make it look good?)
   - workmanship (How well do the materials fit together?)
   - stability (How hard is it to push your tower over?)
   - strength (Can its platform hold up at least 500 g?)

Feature	Tested	Result
strength	✓	• its platform can hold up 510 g

2. Decide what a good or bad result will be for each checklist item.

3. Look carefully at your tower to decide how good its design and workmanship are.

4. Design tests to measure how stable and strong your tower is. Check your test ideas to make sure the tests are fair.

5. Go through your checklist. Test your tower's stability and strength. Record all of your observations and results. How well did your tower support 500 g?

Reflect on Your Results

1. How were the test results on your tower similar to what you expected? How were they different?

2. Which tower feature did you find easiest to judge? Why? Which did you find hardest to judge? Why?

What Did You Learn?

1. What force or forces acted on your tower when you did each test?

2. How do you think you might make your tower stronger or more stable?

SCIENCE IN OUR LIVES

The Leaning Tower of Pisa

The famous Leaning Tower of Pisa was built in Italy over 600 years ago. It is 54 m tall. The tower leans because the foundation was built in clay that is softer on one side than on the other. One side of the tower has sunk more than the other.

The tower leans about 1 mm more each year. It may someday come crashing down. If it does, Italy will lose a world-famous landmark.

To prevent this, engineers buried heavy lead weights on one side of the tower in 1993. The lead weights balance out the leaning. Cables now also support the tower.

INVESTIGATING FURTHER

Take a Tower Trip

Explore the towers in your community. Draw one of the towers you find interesting. Learn as much as you can about it.

- What is it used for?
- How tall is it?
- When was it made?
- What materials were used to make it?
- What shapes does it contain?

Share what you learned with your class.

Did you learn anything about towers that might help you improve your group's tower?

Tower Team

It takes the skills of many people doing many different jobs to build a large structure like a tower. Building requires lots of teamwork.

In Getting Started you will identify some building jobs. In Let's Investigate you will work in a team to build a supertower. In Investigating Further you can use your building and teamwork skills to make a model.

GETTING STARTED

The photo on page 107 shows people working together to build a structure. In a small group, use each other's knowledge and the photo to answer these questions:

- What work are the people in the photo doing?
- What are the names of their jobs?
- What equipment is being used?
- How are the people working as a team?

LET'S INVESTIGATE

You will need
- the building materials you decide on
- any tools you decide to use
- a measuring scale

Your class has been chosen as the design team for a new supertower. You must design and build a tower that supports at least 700 g. It must also have at least one moving part that does a job.

1. Choose one or more people to act as a recorder. These team members should use their science journals to make notes on the project. They will also record any problems you have and how you solve each one.

2. Brainstorm ideas for your supertower. Use everything you have learned about towers to decide on a design for the tower.

3. Make important construction decisions:
   - What materials will we need?
   - What special talents do group members have?
   - How could these talents best be used?
   - What jobs will we need to do?
   - Who will do each job?
   - How long will each job take?

4. Draw a plan of your supertower.

5. Collect and organize your building materials.

6. Perform any tests you think are important on your materials or on your design.

7. Build the supertower!

Reflect on Your Results

1. Did you have any problems when you were building the supertower? If so, how did you solve each one?

2. Did you have any problems working as a team? If so, how did you solve them?

3. What is the strongest part of your tower? What is the weakest? Explain why.

4. How could you improve the strength and stability of your tower?

Use diagrams to help explain any building problems you had.

What Did You Learn?

1. What features help your tower stand up to different kinds of forces?

2. Which part of a tower needs the most strength, the top or the bottom? Why?

INVESTIGATING FURTHER

To find out more about interesting buildings, look for
Super Structures by Phil Wilkinson (Dorling Kindersley: London, UK, 1996).

Drawing Bridges

A drawbridge like the one in this photo is both a structure (something that stands up to forces) and a mechanism (something that moves). What makes it a structure? What makes it a mechanism?

What other structures can you think of that are also mechanisms? Work with a partner to choose one to research. Then, design and make a model of it together.

Thinking About The Builders

1. Name three structures that animals build. Name three structures than humans make. What is similar about animal and human structures?

2. What kind of shapes and features help make structures strong and stable?

3. What features can help a tower hold up a heavy weight?

4. Why is it important to conduct fair tests on structures? What might happen if a structure wasn't tested before people began to use it?

5. Name a lever that you have used, and describe how it works.

6. What things should you do to stay safe when you use tools?

Toy Factory

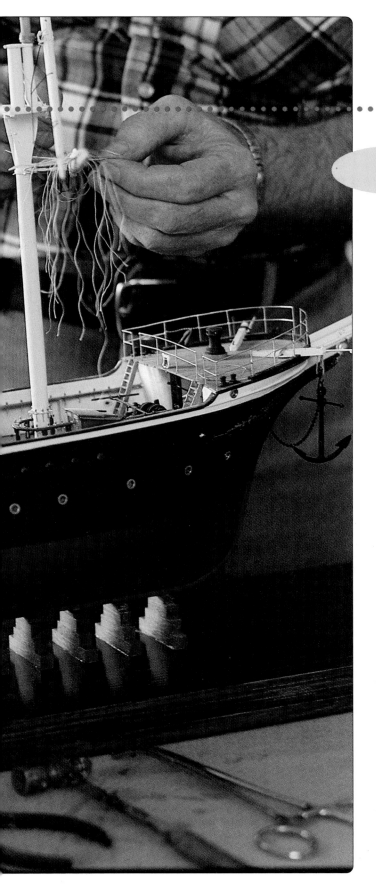

As long as there have been children, children have played with toys. Toys are a lot of fun. Many toy makers use the same scientific ideas to make toys that factories use to make big complex machines.

Complex machines are made of smaller machines that we call simple machines. The inclined plane, the wheel and axle, the pulley, and the lever are all simple machines. Some of your toys may be made from simple machines.

Think about a toy you have seen that moves. What parts of it move? What do you think makes them move?

In Toy Factory you are going to investigate how toys work. Then, your classroom will become a toy factory as you and your classmates make toys that you have designed.

All Kinds of Toys

There are toys that roll and toys that spin. There are toys that you wind up and toys that you push. Think about the toys you play with. How do they move? What makes them move?

In Getting Started you will talk about the toys you know and like to play with. In Let's Observe you will take a closer look at toys that move. In Investigating Further you can show how two similar toys move in different ways.

GETTING STARTED

Look at the toys in the illustration above. Which toy would you choose to play with? Why? Talk with your classmates about what makes toys fun to play with.

LET'S OBSERVE

Let's take a closer look at toys that move.

1. Hold a Toy Day in your classroom.

2. Work in a small group. On a table, display the toys that each of you brought.

3. Look carefully at the toys. What is the same about each one? What is different about each one?

4. Group the toys into categories.

You will need
● a favourite toy brought from home (You might be able to borrow a younger brother's or sister's toy.)

Bring only toys that move or toys that have moving parts. Be sure to label your toy with your name so it will be returned to you.

5. Make a chart in your science journal to show your categories.

6. Compare your group's chart with other groups' charts. As a class, sort all the toys into one chart and display it with the toys for Toy Day.

Your chart could look like this, or you could design one yourself.

Toys We Brought to School	
How they move	Toy
push	car
spin	
wind up	

Reflect on Your Results

1. How easy was it to decide on the categories for your toys?

2. What problems did you have in sorting the toys? How did you solve them?

3. Into which category would you put playground toys? What new categories might you need for these toys?

INFORMATION STATION

Force

Many toys have the ability to move or move other things, but where do they get the power to move?

You can push or pull many toys. This push, provided by you, is called force. Force is a push or pull on an object. The object is called a load. When enough force is used, the load moves. This includes all things that move—toys, bikes, cars, anything!

When you push your toy, you may notice that it takes more effort to get it moving than to keep it moving in the direction you chose. It also takes more effort to stop your toy once it is moving.

Some toys are powered by you pushing or pulling them. Others are powered by you turning a key to tighten a spring. Still others get their power from gravity or from batteries.

Think about your toy. What provides the force that makes it move?

What Did You Learn?

1. What do all toys that move have in common?

2. When you push a toy car across the floor, what makes it move? Read the Information Station to find out what this is called.

3. How do you get the toy car to stop?

4. How can you get the toy car to change direction?

If you want to learn more about how to make toys that move, look for this book: *Make It Work! Machines* by Wendy Baker and Andrew Haslam (Scholastic Canada: Richmond Hill, ON, 1993).

INVESTIGATING FURTHER

You can find a lot of information on the Internet about toys. Use a search engine like Yahoo and type in the name of your favourite toy.

Remote Control Toys

Many toy cars operate by remote control. Find one and examine it closely. How is it different from other toy cars that you push? Think of a way to display the differences and similarities between toy cars that you push and those that you move by remote control. Present your display for Toy Day.

Toys on the Move

Once your toy is moving, it should keep going forever. Think of a toy you know that moves for a long time. What keeps it going? What makes it stop?

Look at the children in this picture. What makes their toboggan stop?

In Getting Started you will feel what happens when two surfaces are rubbed together. In Let's Experiment you will see what happens when a moving object comes in contact with different kinds of surfaces. In Investigating Further you can find out what types of surfaces make the fastest sliders.

GETTING STARTED

Quickly rub the palms of your hands together. How do they feel?

Wet your hands with water and rub a bar of soap between them. Now rub the palms of your hand together. How does this feel different?

LET'S EXPERIMENT

Imagine pushing a friend or a younger brother or sister along in a wagon. Imagine pushing them along in a cardboard box. Which is easier? Why?

This investigation will help you find out why the wagon is an easier way to move another person than the box.

PART 1

You will need
- a brick
- cotton thread

1. Work in groups of two or three. Tie a length of cotton thread around the brick.
2. Pull the brick with the thread. What happens?
3. Talk about how you can pull the brick without breaking the thread. Try your ideas.
4. Record your observations in your science journal.

Reflect on Your Results

1. Why did the thread break when you pulled on it?
2. Which of your ideas about how to pull the brick without breaking the thread worked best? Why?

PART 2

You will need
- a shoebox filled with books, rocks, or anything heavy
- string
- a puller pal
- pencils
- a plastic shopping bag

For instructions on how to make a puller pal, look in the Toolkit on page 242.

1. Work in a small group. Place the filled shoebox on the floor. Attach your puller pal to the shoebox.
2. Using the puller pal, apply enough force to the shoebox to start it moving across the floor. How far down the puller pal scale does the paper clip move? Record the number in your science journal.
3. Talk with your group about ideas to move the shoebox more easily. Try out your ideas and record the results in your science journal.
4. What do you think would happen if you put four or five pencils under the shoebox? Record your answers. Then, put pencils under your shoebox to use as rollers. Pull your shoebox with the puller pal and record in your science journal the number the paper clip reaches.

5. Repeat step 4 using a plastic shopping bag instead of the pencils.

6. What else could you put under the shoebox? Try out your ideas, recording what you think will happen each time.

Reflect on Your Results

1. Was the number on your puller pal the same when the shoebox had been pulled a distance as when the shoebox first started to move? Why do you think this might be?

2. Does it take less force to move the shoebox alone or with pencils underneath it? How do you know?

Force and Friction

Force is needed to start an object moving. But the same amount of force isn't always needed. When there is friction, then more force is necessary. Friction is caused when two surfaces rub together.

When you first tried to move the shoebox along the floor, tiny bumps on the surface of the shoebox got caught on tiny bumps on the surface of the floor, making it hard to move the shoebox. If you can smooth out the tiny bumps, it is easier to move the shoebox.

When you put rollers, like the pencils, under the shoebox, you are doing two things. First, you are moving the bumps on the shoebox away from the bumps on the floor so they can no longer catch on each other. Second, you are putting a round surface to work for you. A round surface doesn't slide. Each part of a round surface only touches the floor once, then rolls away. This is what makes using wheels an easy way to move things.

SCIENCE IN OUR LIVES

Most athletes think about friction when they compete. Athletes who run, such as track-and-field racers or basketball players, make sure the shoes they wear give them a good grip and don't let them slide on the track or court. These athletes want friction to work for them.

Other athletes, such as skaters and skiers, want less friction so that they move faster and more easily along the ice or snow. They make sure their skates and skis are properly cared for so that they are ready for competition.

Think about a sport that you play. How does friction help you? How can it work against you?

SCIENTISTS IN ACTION

The oil in the engine of a car needs to be changed often. If machinery isn't kept properly oiled, friction between moving parts will make the metal so hot that moving parts will stick together or burn out. A thin layer of oil prevents this from happening.

When engines were first used in trains, the train had to be stopped to oil the engine. A man named Elijah McCoy thought that this was a waste of time. McCoy was born in 1844 in Ontario, moved to Scotland to study mechanical engineering, then got a job as a fireman for the Michigan Central Railroad. Part of his job was to oil the engines of the trains.

To save time, McCoy invented a way to oil the train engine while it was still running. His invention was so useful that people refused to buy machinery unless it had the McCoy System for keeping the parts oiled. They would make sure by asking, "Is it the real McCoy?"

What Did You Learn?

1. Why could you not slide very quickly on a slide covered with sandpaper?

2. What type of clothing might help you slide more easily?

3. List three times when you would want friction to work for you.

INVESTIGATING FURTHER

Before you hold your Slippery Slope Race, guess which cookie sheet will have the fastest sliders.

Slippery Slopes

Test several substances on a cookie sheet to see which surface causes the least amount of friction. Use a small object as your slider, such as a wooden block. You could put vegetable oil, sandpaper, or ice on the cookie sheet— or anything else you can think of. Get several of your classmates together and hold a Slippery Slope Race!

What's Inside?

When you want to find out how something works, you can take it apart. What do you do if you can't take it apart? How would a scientist deal with this problem?

In **Getting Started** you will make scientific observations about a mystery box. In **Let's Investigate** you will design an experiment to find out what's inside a sealed can and then do the same to some toys. In **Investigating Further** you can make a speedy spool.

GETTING STARTED

Carefully examine four mystery boxes. You may not open them or flatten them. You may look at them, shake them, and smell them. Try any other method of observation that will help you find out what's inside the container. How can you find out what's inside?

This chart might help you organize your observations.

Mystery Boxes		
Container number	Observations	What I think is inside
1	makes a swishy sound	
2	very heavy	

LET'S INVESTIGATE

You will need
- an empty can
- a sealed can provided by your teacher

Often a scientist has to find out how something works without taking it apart. In this investigation you are going to follow the same procedures a scientist would when presented with a scientific mystery.

PART 1

1. What do you think will happen when you roll an empty can along a level surface like the floor of your classroom or a kitchen counter? Write your answer in your science journal.

2. Test your answers. Record your results in your science journal.

3. Now, carefully look at the can your teacher has given you. How is it the same as the one you just tested? How is it different? Write in your science journal what you think will happen when you roll it along a level surface.

4. Test the can. Record your results in your science journal.

5. What other ways can you test the can to find out what's inside? (Remember, you can't open it.) Write down your ideas and then try them.

Reflect on Your Results

1. Compare rolling the two cans. What surprised you about the results?

2. What do you think caused the different results?

3. How did performing tests on the can help you figure out what was inside?

Make sure you have permission to take apart a toy before you do so.

Drawings are a big help when making observations.

PART 2

1. Examine a toy the same way you did the mystery boxes and the sealed can. Write your observations in your science journal. Include your ideas about how the toy works.

2. Design a test that will help you find out how the toy works. Perform your test and write in your science journal how you think the toy works.

3. Now, carefully begin to take the toy apart. Continue to make observations as you remove each part.

4. After you have taken the toy apart, write in your science journal how you think it works.

Reflect on Your Results

1. What did you learn about how the toy works before taking it apart?

2. How was the inside of the toy similar to what you expected? How was it different?

3. How did taking the toy apart help you in your observations?

What Did You Learn?

1. You are helping to make dinner and you find three cans in the cupboard that have no labels. How can you find out what's inside each one without opening the cans?

2. Look at the inside of the sealed can you used earlier. Explain how the can works now that you know what's inside. When you roll the can, where does the force come from to make it roll back?

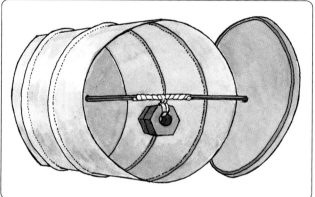

▲ The inside of your can might look like this.

3. There are lots of toys that you wind up to make them move or do something. What things that are not toys can you think of that work the same way?

4. Why is it important to always ask questions when you are doing science? Why is it important to write down your observations?

SCIENCE IN OUR LIVES

When you want to find out what is inside something and you can't take it apart, here are some steps you can follow.

1. Look at the object.
2. Take measurements and write down your observations.
3. Compare it to something you are familiar with.
4. Do some research to find out what might be inside it.
5. Guess what might be inside.
6. Design a simple experiment to test your guess.
7. Come to a conclusion.

Scientists often follow steps like these when they are trying to find an answer to a question.

INVESTIGATING FURTHER

Speedy Spools

A speedy spool is a toy you can make that uses stored-up energy, like the mystery can.

Take a wooden or plastic thread spool and follow the instructions in this diagram to make your speedy spool.

Straighten one end of a paper clip to push the elastic band through the spool. To wind up your speedy spool, rotate the paper clip. Test your spool a couple of times to make sure you are satisfied with its performance. How can you make your speedy spool go farther? Hold a speedy spool race with your classmates!

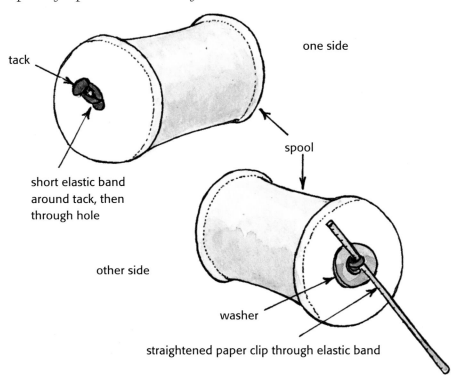

tack

one side

short elastic band around tack, then through hole

spool

other side

washer

straightened paper clip through elastic band

1. Make sure the rubber band is a little bit shorter than the length of the spool.

2. The short end of the paper clip must not go past the edge of the spool's rim.

Try making a speedy spool out of something larger, like an empty aluminum pop can. How can you make it work?

Spin Away

Not all toys need to be pulled or pushed in a straight line to move. Some you can spin. Some you can wind up. How do the toys and rides in this picture move?

In **Getting Started** you will make a simple wind-up toy. In **Let's Investigate** you will make a toy that spins. In **Investigating Further** you can design an experiment to test your toy.

A button with more weight on the rim than on the centre works best.

GETTING STARTED

Have you ever seen a buzz-button? A buzz-button is a toy that your grandparents probably made to play with.

To make your own, take a large coat button and about 1 m of fine string or strong thread. Thread the string through two holes in the button, and tie the ends in a knot so that the button hangs in the centre of the loop.

To make the buzz-button work, put a loop of the string around each thumb and hold your arms out in front of you. Whirl the button on the string to wind it up, then pull the string hard with each thumb. The button should twirl around and spin itself up again, rewinding itself. This will continue as long as you move your thumbs together and pull them apart. (You can use your fingers, too!)

The button and the string make a buzzing sound as they wind and rewind, which gives the toy its name. What do you think creates the sound? What provides the force to make the button spin?

LET'S INVESTIGATE

Here's another spinning toy you can make. A top is one of the oldest toys. Children around the world have played with tops for centuries.

1. Glue two paper plates together, placing them so the rims are facing each other.

2. Draw a line across the widest part of your paper plates. Draw a second line that crosses the first line across the widest part of the plate to make an X. The centre of the X is the centre of your paper plates.

3. Push the sharpened pencil, point first, through the centre of your paper plates. Glue the pencil in place.

4. Spin your top, placing a piece of paper under it first. You may have to practise to get the right touch.

5. Decorate your top. Use markers to make an interesting pattern. How does the pattern look while the top is spinning?

6. Try your top on different surfaces such as plastic, sandpaper, wood, concrete, or carpet.

7. Record in your science journal how well your top spins on each type of surface you try.

Strong paper plates will work best.

You can make a chart to record what surface you are testing and how long your top spins on it.

8. What happens when you change the length of the pencil? Try it and record your observations.

9. What happens if the pencil is not pushed in at the exact centre of the paper plates? Try it and record the results in your science journal.

10. Design other tests for your top, changing only one thing at a time. Remember to keep your test fair. Record all of your observations in your science journal.

Reflect on Your Results

1. What provides the force for your spinning top?

2. On what surface does your top spin the best? Why does the surface make a difference to how well your top spins?

3. Which change that you made to your top made the biggest difference in how well your top spins?

INFORMATION STATION

Testing Variables

When scientists do experiments, they often do more than one test, changing one thing about the test each time. The things they can change are called variables. When you changed the length of the pencil in your top, you changed one variable.

It is important to change only one variable at a time. If you change more than one, you will not know which change affected your results. If you had changed both the length of the pencil and the surface on which your top spins, you wouldn't have known which change made your top spin better or worse.

What Did You Learn?

1. How was the force that made the buzz-button spin different from the force that made your top spin?

2. What did you learn from your spinning-top experiment by changing only one variable at a time?

INVESTIGATING FURTHER

Spinning Tops

Design another experiment to see which top spins longest. You can change any variable you like as long as you change only one variable at a time. For example, you can test your top with a mass attached to the paper plate. You can try different positions for the mass. Or you can try another idea of your own. Hold a Spinning Top Jamboree once you have found the top design that works the best.

Pulleys, Pulleys, Pulleys

Look at the machines on this page. Which ones look familiar to you? What do some toys do that is similar to these machines?

In **Getting Started** you will examine toy pulleys. In **Let's Investigate** you will use pulleys to move a load. In **Investigating Further** you can look for pulleys in the world around you.

GETTING STARTED

If you can, collect some toy cranes and examine them.
What do cranes do? Where is the force applied to move
a load? Where is the load?

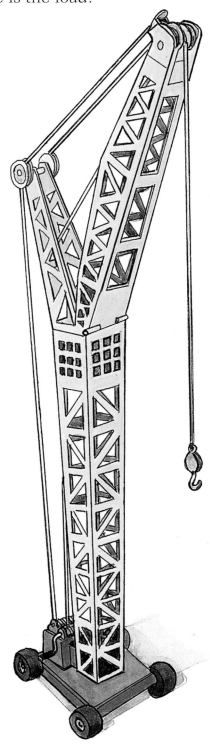

A crane uses pulleys to lift heavy loads. Work in a small group for this investigation and learn more about pulleys.

You will need
- 2 m length of cord or fishing line
- a pail or a basket with a handle
- sand, marbles, or pebbles
- a puller pal

You can make a puller pal using the instructions on page 242 in the Toolkit.

1. Put some marbles, sand, or pebbles in the pail.

2. Use the puller pal to lift the pail by the handle. Write in your science journal how far the puller pal stretches.

3. Tie the cord to a doorknob or coat hook.

4. Loop the cord through the pail's handle, then over the doorknob again. Tie the end to your puller pal.

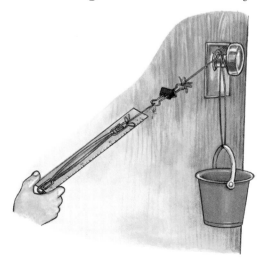

5. Use your puller pal to pull the cord and lift the pail. Write in your science journal how far the puller pal stretches.

1. When did your puller pal stretch more—when you lifted the pail using a pulley or when you lifted the pail without using a pulley? Why do you think that happened?

2. How do pulleys help when you have a load to lift?

What Did You Learn?

1. What supplied the force for your pulley? What was the load?

2. What is similar between your pulley and the pulleys in the photos on page 136 at the beginning of this learning event?

INVESTIGATING FURTHER

Pulleys All Around

Where can you find pulleys outside? Look for examples and draw pictures of them in your science journal. You can find more examples of pulleys in a library. Look for books about machines to help you.

Rollers and Ramps

Imagine you are riding on a roller coaster. A motor is used to take you to the top of the first hill. Where does the force to make you roll forward come from? Which toys use force in the same way?

In Getting Started you will talk about ramps. In Let's Experiment you will learn how ramps affect force. In Investigating Further you can use what you learned about ramps to design a bobsled run.

GETTING STARTED

Look at the ramps on page 140. How are they the same? Are any of them used for a different purpose than the others? How are these ramps different?

LET'S EXPERIMENT

When you push a toy car, the force comes from your push. When you use a ramp, the force comes from gravity pulling on the toy car. Compare these ramps.

1. Cut the paper towel rolls in half.

2. Tape several half rolls together so you have three ramps of different lengths. Label your ramps one, two, and three.

3. Roll a marble down ramp 1. Measure the distance it rolls.

4. Roll the same marble down ramps 2 and 3. Measure the distance it rolls each time.

You will need
- several paper towel rolls
- marbles of different sizes
- a measuring tape or metre stick
- sticky tape

5. Repeat steps 3 and 4 for each different-sized marble you have. Record all your measurements on a chart in your science journal.

Distance a Marble Rolled			
	Short ramp	Medium ramp	Long ramp
small marble medium marble large marble			

6. Design other tests for your marbles and ramps. For example, the ramps could be placed on sandpaper or carpet. Design a chart to record the results of each test.

Reflect on Your Results

1. How does the length of the ramp affect the distance the marble travels?

2. How does the size of the marble affect the distance it travels?

3. What happens if the marble has to roll over a rough surface?

What Did You Learn?

1. What force made your marbles travel down the ramps? How is this force different from pushing your race car with your hand?

2. What did you change in your marble experiment? What stayed the same?

3. How does a rough surface affect your ramp? What would happen if the surface was very rough?

4. Will the marble roll farther on a hard floor or on carpet? Explain why.

INVESTIGATING FURTHER

Let's Go Bobsledding!

Use the same idea of building ramps out of paper towel rolls to build a bobsled run. You can use books or modelling clay to raise one end of your ramp, and extra pieces of construction paper to strengthen the paper towel rolls and add curves. Use marbles, or design a bobsled using marbles and a small cardboard box, such as a matchbox. You may want to experiment to come up with the best bobsled design. Hold a bobsled derby!

Magnetic Power

Magnets can be fun toys. You can use them to pick things up and also to make toys move. How do you think that might work? What are some toys that use magnets? Which toys in this picture use magnets?

In **Getting Started** you will make a magnetic puppet. In **Let's Investigate** you will use magnetic force to race toy cars. In **Investigating Further** you can test the difference between pushing and pulling with a magnet. You can also see how distance changes magnetic force.

GETTING STARTED

Follow these directions to make your own magnetic toy.

1. Draw and cut out a head and body for your puppet. Make it about 6 cm long.

2. Link three or four paper clips together for each arm and leg. Use sticky tape to attach them to the body of the puppet.

3. Attach a string to the head of the puppet and tape the string to a stiff piece of paper like a notebook cover. Ask a friend to hold up the paper, then stand behind the paper with your magnet to make your puppet dance!

You will need
- several small toy cars
- nails, safety pins, or paper clips
- poster board
- markers or crayons
- magnets
- metre sticks

You can also set up your race track on two piles of books.

Here's another toy you can make with magnets. Work in groups of two or three to use magnetic force to power race cars.

1. Draw a race track on a sheet of poster board. Make it a fairly large oval.

2. Set up your race track on two desks across an aisle. You should be able to reach under the track. Tape metre sticks to the desks first for extra support.

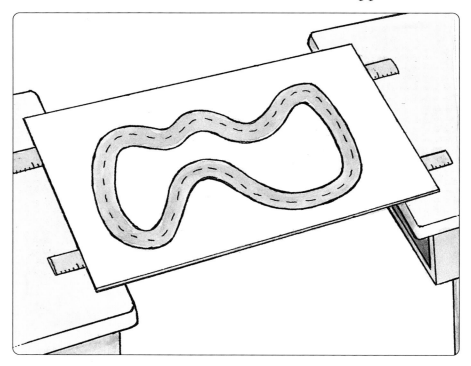

3. Tape a nail, safety pin, or paper clip to the bottom of each car.

4. Stick a piece of masking tape to each car and give it a number.

5. Hold the magnet below the poster board underneath your car, then pull it along. You might want to have a practice run first.

6. It's off to the races! Race your cars two at a time.

Reflect on Your Results

1. What provided the force to move your race cars?

2. How might you improve the performance of your race car?

What Did You Learn?

1. What kind of object is attracted to a magnet? How do you know?

INVESTIGATING FURTHER

Magnetic Racing Cars

Change your race car so it has a magnet attached to it. Attach a second magnet to a metre stick and experiment with ways to move your race car. What way works best?

Toy Engineers

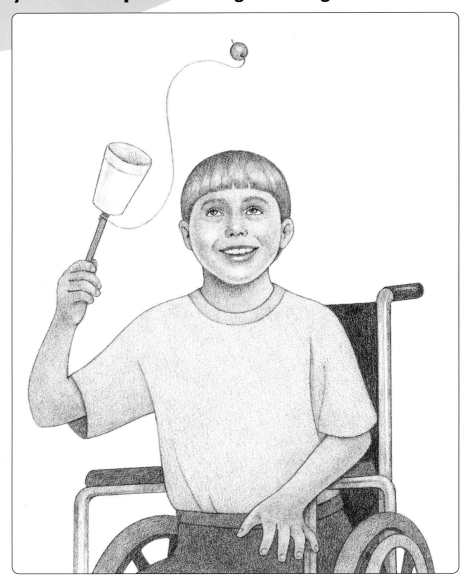

Here is your chance to use what you have learned about toys to design your own toy. You are a toy engineer.

In Getting Started you will see how a plan can help you as you design your toy. In Let's Build you will design a toy of your choice. In Investigating Further you can take part in a design challenge.

GETTING STARTED

When toy engineers design a toy, they first draw a plan. This plan gives them a record of their design. If it's a good design, a toy factory can use the same plan to make copies of the toy.

Use this plan to make the toy shown in this illustration.

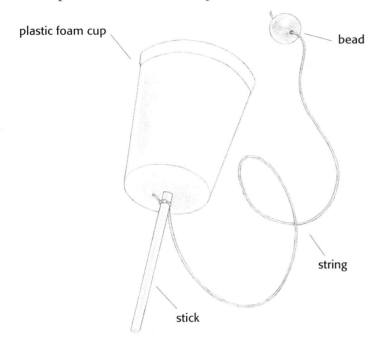

plastic foam cup

bead

string

stick

LET'S BUILD

Build your own toy with moving parts. Your toy must have at least one moving part and it must be made of materials that are easy to find.

1. Work in a small group. Brainstorm ideas for what your toy should do and write them down on a large piece of paper.

2. Choose one idea and work with your group to draw a plan. If part of it doesn't look like it will work, draw it a different way. Once you are satisfied with your plan, draw a final version in your science journal.

You will need
- materials to build your toy
- a large sheet of paper

3. Make a list of the materials and equipment that you will need to build your toy.

4. Collect the things you need. If you cannot find one thing, you may have to change your plan to use materials that you can find.

5. Build your toy.

6. Test your toy.

7. Discuss what changes you can make to improve your toy. Mark the changes on your plan.

8. Change your toy to make it better.

9. Hold a Toy Display to show how your toy works.

Reflect on Your Results

1. What have you learned about toys that helped you design your own toy?

2. How did your plan help make building the toy easier?

3. How did your group decide which toy to build?

SCIENTISTS IN ACTION

There is science behind how every toy works. Would your toy work as well in space as it does on earth?

Dr. Carolyn Sumners wanted to find out how toys would work in space, so she convinced NASA to send some toys up in the space shuttle.

On April 12, 1985, the space shuttle *Discovery* took 11 toys into space, where there is no gravity. The scientists on board spent several hours testing toys to understand the effects of gravity on them.

The toys worked very well in the zero gravity environment. Some even worked better in space than on earth. The yo-yo and the paddle ball, for example, were able to move in all directions equally well. How do you think some of your toys would work in space?

If you want to learn more about toys in space, look for this book:
Toys in Space: Exploring Science With the Astronauts
by Carolyn Sumners (McGraw Hill: New York, U.S., 1997).

What Did You Learn?

1. What can scientists learn from toys?

2. What do you think a toy engineer does? What do you think would be the most difficult part of the job?

3. Write an explanation of how the toy you built works. Include in your explanation where the force is and where the load is.

INVESTIGATING FURTHER

Engineering Challenge

Challenge a classmate to make a toy. Make up rules for the challenge. For example, the toy can only move forward, or the toy must have wheels, or the toy must be made only of paper. You can write the different rules on pieces of paper and put them in a bowl for your classmate to choose from.

1. List four things that moving toys can get their power from.

2. Draw a toy that can move. Use arrows to label the force that makes your toy move and the load that is moved.

3. What change could you make to help this toy car below roll down this ramp more quickly?

4. How could you make the car roll down the ramp more slowly?

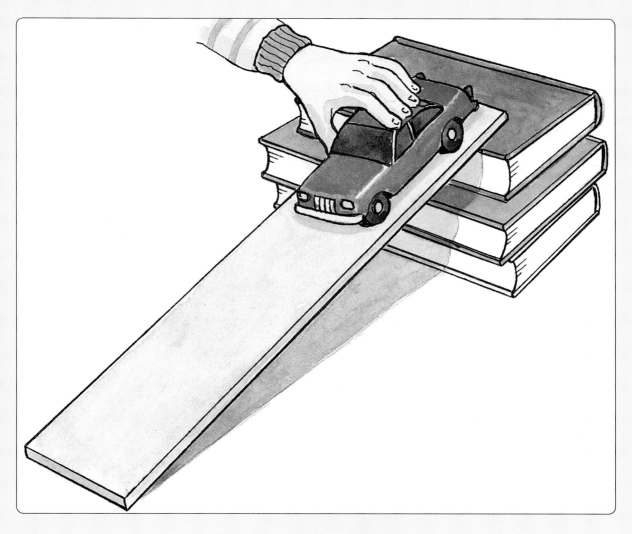

Mud and Dirt

Soil means different things to different people. Gardeners and farmers are concerned with how soil affects growing plants. Soil scientists are interested in the characteristics of soil and in soil as a home for living things. Engineers see soil as part of the earth's surface where homes, bridges, and roads can be built.

There are different types of soil that cover our planet. In this unit, you will examine some of these types and look at how water affects soil. You will also explore ways to protect the earth's soil.

Where have you noticed soil? How have you played with it? How have you used it? Answer these questions in your science journal. When you finish this unit, look back at your answers. What new information can you add to your science journal?

Beneath Our Feet

What is soil made of? How do you know? Take a closer look at some soil to find out. In **Getting Started** you will think about the living and non-living things in soil. In **Let's Investigate** you will look closely at some soil and identify its different parts. In **Investigating Further** you can find out what makes soil good for growing plants.

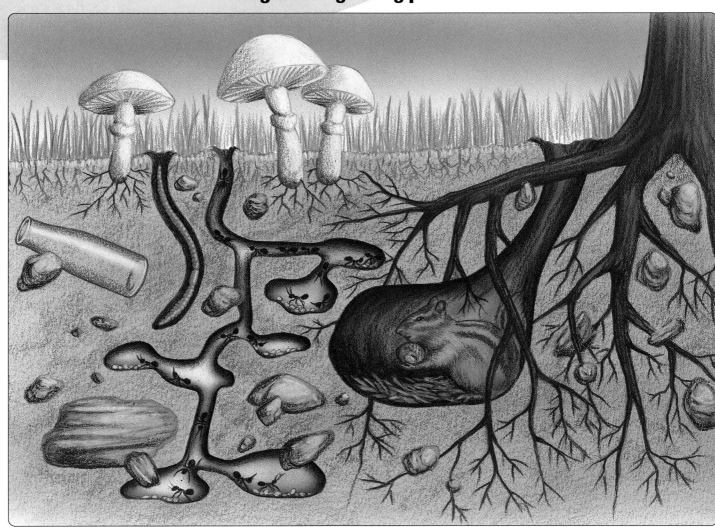

GETTING STARTED

Just under your feet is a whole world of living and non-living things. What do you think they are? How can you find out? Discuss your ideas with a classmate.

LET'S INVESTIGATE

Find out for yourself what is inside soil! Look for a safe place to collect some soil that will do no harm to any plants or animals.

1. Collect a soil sample and put it in your container. Put a label on it that says where you found the sample.

2. Empty the soil sample onto the sheet of newsprint. Pick the soil apart using the stick. Separate what you find into different piles, putting the same type of material in each pile.

Be sure to wear gloves to protect your hands when you collect soil. Check with your teacher about safe places to collect your samples.

You will need
- a shovel or trowel
- gloves
- a 500-mL container
- a label
- a sheet of white newsprint
- a craft stick
- a magnifier (optional)

For instructions on how to make a simple magnifier, look in the Toolkit on page 239.

Keep a record of what you found in your soil sample. Draw pictures of the different piles. Label each pile.

A sieve might help you as you sort your sample into different piles.

3. Count and keep a record of the number of living and non-living things you find.

4. Continue sorting the soil into as many different piles as you wish, but remember to keep the same type of material in each pile.

5. When you have finished, look at a classmate's soil sample to see how it was sorted. See if you can decide what sorting rules were used.

Reflect on Your Results

1. Which pile from your soil sample is the biggest? Why?

2. Make a list of your piles, starting with the biggest pile and ending with the smallest.

3. Compare your list with others in the class. Which lists are the most like yours? Why?

What Did You Learn?

1. Soil samples taken from different areas will be made up of different materials. How was your soil sample different from those of your classmates?

2. If you compared a soil sample from under a tree with a soil sample from a parking lot, what differences might you find?

3. Where did the soil samples with the most organic material come from? Read the Information Station to find out what *organic* means.

4. Soil scientists keep very careful records of where they find their soil samples. Why do you think they do this?

Soil Detectives

As you separated your soil sample into piles, you saw many different things. Your soil sample may have looked like the one shown on the right.

The large pile of dirt and stones is full of inorganic material. These materials are called inorganic because they are not alive.

Leaves, roots, sticks, grass, and twigs are examples of organic material. Organic material in soil is made up of things that are still living or were once alive.

Sometimes it is difficult to separate all the organic material out of the soil. This is because it is already in the process of decaying. This partly decayed organic material is called humus. After it has completely decayed, it becomes part of the soil itself. Look for grass in your soil sample. It may be only partly decayed and may be difficult to pull away from the soil.

Soil is also home to many living things. Some are easy to see, like ants, beetles, and earthworms. Others, like fungi and bacteria, are so small we can only look at them with the help of a microscope. What living things did you see in your soil sample?

Look at the piles you sorted your soil sample into. Decide which piles are organic, or living materials, and which are inorganic, or non-living materials.

INVESTIGATING FURTHER

If you want to learn more about mud and dirt, look for this book:

The Amazing Dirt Book by Paulette Bourgeois (Kids Can Press: Toronto, ON, 1990).

New and Improved Soil

Gardeners take care to create just the right mix of ingredients in the soil they use to grow plants. Look at a bag of soil for house plants that you can buy in a garden store. What ingredients are listed on the outside of the bag? How is the soil inside the bag similar to, or different from, your soil sample?

SCIENCE IN OUR LIVES

Plants grow better in soil that has lots of humus in it because it contains more nutrients than other types of soil.

Gardeners sometimes use compost to make humus to add to their garden soil. You can make your own compost heap by following these instructions.

1. Place a layer of soil on the bottom of a plastic tub.
2. Cover the soil with a layer of organic material such as grass clippings, leaves, and fruit and vegetable peelings.
3. Place another layer of soil on top.
4. Keep your container outside, in the sun if possible.
5. Continue to add organic material and soil. Stir the contents every week or so.
6. After a few months, you should have a container full of dark, rich humus to spread on a garden.

A Closer Look at Soil

Soil comes in many different colours. Why do you think this might be? Often, one type of soil feels very different from another. What does this tell you about soil?

In Getting Started you will look at pictures of three different types of soil and will talk about them. In Let's Observe you will feel the three different types of soil. In Investigating Further you can find out why soil comes in many different colours.

GETTING STARTED

Look carefully at these photos of three types of soil. Which soil types do you recognize? Talk about what you think they might be.

▲ soil A

▲ soil B

▲ soil C

You will need
- 3 soil samples (loam, clay, and sand)
- 3 sheets of white newsprint
- a magnifier (optional)

For instructions on how to make a simple magnifier, look in the Toolkit on page 239.

What makes one type of soil different from another? What makes them similar? Work in a small group to take a closer look at three different types of soil.

1. Empty one soil sample onto a sheet of newsprint.
2. Examine the soil and describe it. Use the following questions to help you.
   - What colours can you see in the soil?
   - How does the soil feel?
   - Take a handful of soil. Does it stick together or fall apart?
   - What does it smell like?
   - Is it heavy or light?

3. If you have a magnifier, use it to observe the soil.

4. Write your observations in your science journal. Return the soil to its container.

5. Repeat steps 1 to 4 for the remaining two soil samples.

Make a chart in your science journal to record your observations about your soil samples.

Sample 1	Sample 2	Sample 3
-clumpy -medium brown -smells damp -a little heavy		

Reflect on Your Results

1. Compare your notes with those of other members of your group.

2. How did the questions help you to make your observations?

3. What types of soil might your samples be? Why?

Wash your hands with soap and warm water after you handle soil.

INFORMATION STATION

Soil Types

Soil is identified by its colour and texture. Soil can be many colours. Look at your soil samples. What colours are they?

Loam is a loose, crumbly soil that is found in gardens and in farmers' fields. It is rich in nutrients that help plants grow, and is usually dark brown or black (soil A on page 161).

Soil that is medium brown is probably clay. Clay feels heavy and slippery when it is wet and looks stiff and clumpy when it is dry. Clay is easy to mould when it is wet. It becomes hard when it is dry (soil C on page 161). ▶

Sand feels light and is easy to pour. It comes in many colours and is most often found in deserts and on beaches (soil B on page 161).

The texture of a soil depends on the size of its particles. When you rub sand between your fingers, it feels gritty. Loam feels slightly rough, while clay feels slippery and lumpy.

Colour and texture are properties, or features, of soil. Soil can be identified by its properties. This is because each type of soil has its own properties.

What Did You Learn?

1. In your science journal, write the properties of each type of soil.

2. Read the Information Station to help you label each soil sample as loam, clay, or sand.

3. What helped you decide the type of each soil sample?

4. Which soil sample were you able to recognize quickly? Why?

INVESTIGATING FURTHER

A Rainbow of Sand

You have probably seen white sand in playground sandboxes and in egg timers. Have you ever seen black or pink sand?

Some beaches on the Hawaiian Islands have black sand. Find out why the sand is black. (Hint: The Hawaiian Islands were once volcanoes.)

There are pink beaches on Prince Edward Island. Look in an encyclopedia, on a CD-ROM, or on the Internet to find out why that sand is pink.

Just Add Water

Until now, you have been examining soil when it is dry. If you add water to a pile of soil, you get mud. Sometimes mud can be fun, but mud can also cause a lot of problems. What problems can you think of that are caused by mud?

In Getting Started you will think about where water goes when it rains. In Let's Experiment you will see what happens to different types of soil when you add water to them. In Investigating Further you can find out how one plant has adapted to its dry environment.

GETTING STARTED

When it rains, we see raindrops dripping down windows and noses. When we look out the window, we see rain making puddles on the streets and on the sidewalks. However, look out onto a field or a park the next time it rains. Where does the water go? Discuss your ideas.

LET'S EXPERIMENT

You will need
- a clear plastic bottle with the bottom removed
- a wide-mouthed jar
- 200 mL each of dry loam, clay, and sand
- a paper coffee filter
- a measuring cup
- water

You might enjoy reading about a boy who discovered a one-of-a-kind item to sell. Look for this book:
Mud for Sale
by Brenda Nelson
(Houghton Mifflin: Boston, MA, U.S., 1989).

What happens when you add water to loam, clay, and sand? What do these different types of soil look like when they turn into mud? How do they feel? Will water flow through them in exactly the same way? How could you find out?

1. Place the plastic bottle upside down on top of the wide-mouthed jar.
2. Measure 200 mL of loam into the coffee filter.
3. Gather the edges of the filter together. Place the filter inside the plastic bottle.
4. Pour 100 mL of water into the bottle.
5. Measure the amount of water that pours through the filter into the jar.
6. How does the soil feel? Does it feel lighter or heavier than it did before you poured the water on it?

7. Repeat steps 1 to 6 with the clay and the sand. Record
your observations about each type of soil on a chart in
your science journal. Your chart could look like the
one below, or you could design your own.

Type of soil	What I observed	Amount of water in jar

Reflect on Your Results

1. Read what you wrote in your chart.

2. Which soil did water flow through most easily? least easily?

3. All three soil samples became wet after water was added to them. How did they feel? Which soil felt the wettest or the heaviest?

What Did You Learn?

1. Look at the third column of your chart. Which soil allowed the greatest amount of water to pass through it? Why did this soil let so much water through?

2. Which soil allowed the least amount of water to pass through it? Where did the rest of the water go? Why did this soil hold so much water?

3. Read the Information Station. Name three properties of soil. Now that you know how much water is absorbed by loam, clay, and sand, which type of soil would you choose to grow plants in? Why?

4. Suppose you poured much more water onto each soil sample. What do you think would happen?

Absorbing Soils

You already know about two properties of soil—colour and texture. The new property you have just discovered is called water absorption. This is the soil's ability to hold water.

Soil is able to hold water because there are spaces between the particles of soil. When water is poured over soil, it finds these spaces and some of it stays there.

The particles in clay soil are so close together that very little water can fit in the spaces. When water is poured over clay, most of it runs off. Very little water stays in the soil.

Sand particles are loose, with lots of space in between. When water is poured over sand, some of it stays in the spaces, but much of it passes right through. Sandy soil is used in places where good drainage is needed, for example, under road beds.

The particles in loam are not as close together as in clay, nor as far apart as in sand. Loam holds the most water of the three soil types, and the least amount of water will pass through.

SCIENCE IN OUR LIVES

Floods occur when too much rain falls and the soil is unable to absorb all of the water. Canada has had many floods, unfortunately. They occur most often in spring when heavy rains add to the melting snow. In the spring of 1997, the Red River in Manitoba overflowed its banks. More than 800 farms were covered in water, and thousands of people had to leave their homes. ▶

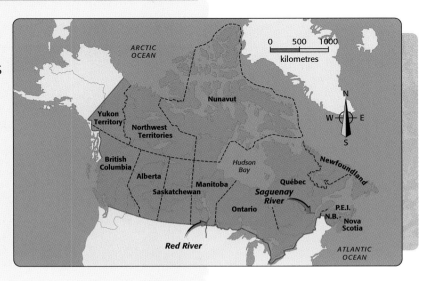

In 1996, a huge summer rainstorm caused the Saguenay River in Québec to flood its banks. More than 15 000 people had to leave their homes to be safe from flooded rivers and mudslides.

Dams and dikes are built to help control floods. People also use sandbags to build temporary dikes and dams. However, sooner or later, these sandbag dikes leak. Why do they always leak? (Hint: Think about what happened when you poured water over sand in your experiment.)

INVESTIGATING FURTHER

The Cactus

Deserts have sandy soil and very few plants. The cactus is one plant that has learned how to survive in the desert. Did you know that the cactus grows in Canada? You can find cacti on the southern prairies of Alberta, Saskatchewan, and Manitoba. The pincushion cactus and three types of prickly pear grow there. Prickly pear cacti also grow at the southern tip of Ontario.

How does the cactus get enough water to live?

Setting Soils

Y̲ou now know what happens to different types of soil when water is poured over them. Water also plays an important part in making and moving soil. How do you think it does this?

Much of the earth's soil is put in place by moving water. In Getting Started you will talk about how layers of soil are formed. In Let's Experiment you will add water to different types of soil and see what happens. In Investigating Further you can learn how the type of soil found in water can affect the colour of that water.

GETTING STARTED

Look at the soil and rocks in this picture. Why do you think they look like this? Suggest how they might have been formed.

What do you think happens when soil is mixed with water? What happens when you throw a handful of pebbles into a river or a lake? What happens when the pebbles are mixed with sand? Find out what happens when water is added to different types of soil.

You will need
- small amounts of loam, clay, and sand
- 3 large glass jars with lids
- water
- a spoon

PART 1

1. Put four or five spoonfuls of loam in the jar.

2. Add water to the jar until it is almost full. Put on the lid and shake the jar until the soil and water are mixed.

3. Put the jar in a place where it won't be disturbed for a day or two.

4. Repeat steps 1 to 3 with the clay and the sand.

Reflect on Your Results

1. What did your jars look like immediately after you shook them? What did they look like after 30 minutes?

2. What did they look like the next day?

3. What differences were there among the three jars of soil and water? What do you think is the reason for these differences?

PART 2

1. Put three spoonfuls each of loam, clay, and sand in the jar.

2. Add water to the jar until it is almost full. Put on the lid and shake the jar until the soil and water are mixed.

3. Put the jar in a place where it won't be disturbed for a day or two.

4. Predict what your jar of soil and water will look like after a day.

You will need
- small amounts of loam, clay, and sand
- a large glass jar with a lid
- water
- a spoon

Reflect on Your Results

1. What did your jar look like immediately after you shook it? What did it look like after 30 minutes?

2. What did it look like the next day?

3. What do you think happened? How close was your prediction?

What Did You Learn?

1. Write about how the soil's texture and the amount of water it absorbed account for what happened to each jar of soil and water.

2. Different types of soil have different amounts of space between their particles. You learned this when you read about water absorption on page 164. Different types of soil also have different sizes of particles, and this affects how soil reacts with water. Why did the jar with water and clay look different from the jar with water and loam?

3. How do you explain the results of the jar that contained all three types of soil? Where have you seen this type of pattern before?

INVESTIGATING FURTHER

Soiled Water

Look at the lake in this picture. Why do you think it is that colour? (Hint: It has to do with the type of soil found nearby.)

Roots on the Move

Plants grow in gardens, in fields, in hanging baskets, and in water. We see part of a plant above the soil or water.

If we could look under the earth, we would see the plant's roots. Roots hold the plant in place in the soil. Roots also collect and store the water and nutrients that plants need to survive.

In **Getting Started** you will predict what type of soil roots like best. In **Let's Investigate** you will watch seeds as they grow roots and will observe the effects of different types of soil on the roots. In **Investigating Further** you can see what happens to the roots as the plant continues to grow above the soil.

GETTING STARTED

Think about the three types of soil—loam, clay, and sand. Which type of soil do you think roots like best? How do you know? How can you find out if your answer is correct?

LET'S INVESTIGATE

One way to find out which soil roots like best is to test them. Plant seeds in loam, clay, and sand to see what happens. This investigation will take about a week to complete.

1. Place a different type of soil in each of the three jars.

2. Use the spoon to help push three seeds into the soil in each jar. Make sure you can see the seeds through the side of the jar.

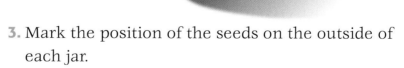

You will need
- 9 mung bean seeds
- some loam, clay, and sand
- 3 small glass jars or clear plastic containers
- a ruler
- a spoon
- a marker
- water

3. Mark the position of the seeds on the outside of each jar.

4. Sprinkle a few drops of water over your seeds every day.

5. For five days, observe how your seeds change. Measure the changes. Draw a picture of your seeds each day, and write down your observations in your science journal.

Comparing the Growth of Mung Beans

Number of days	In loam	In clay	In sand
1			
2			

Reflect on Your Results

1. After five days, look at the marks you made when you planted your seeds. Where are the seeds now? Why did they move in this direction?

2. Describe how the roots look in each of the three types of soil. What do you notice?

What Did You Learn?

1. Plants will go around materials in the soil as they try to reach the surface. In which type of soil did you notice this happening?

2. Which of your seeds grew roots that had to travel a great distance to keep the plant upright? Why do you think the roots grew this way? (Hint: When the particles in soil are far apart, the roots have to travel farther.)

3. How did the different types of soil affect the way your seeds grew? Which type of soil did you feel was best for your seeds to grow in? Write the answer in your science journal.

4. Gardeners and farmers prefer a loam soil to grow their plants in. Use your results to explain why.

5. Read the Information Station to find out what kind of root your mung bean seeds have.

INFORMATION STATION

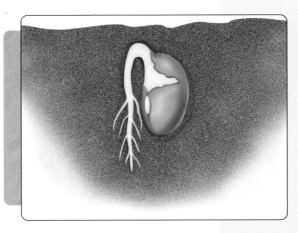

Roots

There are two main types of roots. The mung bean you planted has a fibrous root. As a mung bean grows, many thin roots form, with smaller branches of roots growing out from them.

After the seed has been planted and watered, the root pushes out of the seed. The coating on the seed then splits, and root hairs appear. Finally, the upper part of the root pushes out of the soil and pulls the rest of the seed with it. What did the upper root turn into after it pushed itself out of the soil? ▶

What did you notice began to appear?

The other type of root is a tap root. Unlike a mung bean, which has many roots, a dandelion has one main root, or tap root, that is larger than all the other roots. A carrot is another plant with a tap root. Can you think of any other vegetables that have tap roots?

Look at the picture of the dandelion and its roots.

SCIENTISTS IN ACTION

We interviewed Donald Vaughan, a soybean farmer, to find out more about plants and soil.

What do you grow on your farm?
Corn, wheat, and soybeans.

Why won't soybeans grow very well in clay?
Clay contains less organic matter than loam. Organic matter helps soils hold moisture that sticks small particles together to form large particles. Plant root systems are usually smaller in fine clay soils.

What, if anything, grows well in clay? Why does it grow well?
Crops like hay, clover, and alfalfa produce deep roots that help break up compacted clay soils.

Cultivating soil breaks it up for planting, but can soil be cultivated too much?
Yes, soil that is cultivated too much compacts and usually crusts after a pounding rainstorm. Young plants can't push through the crust, and plant roots do not grow as large in compacted soils.

Read about how to make a pictograph in the Toolkit on page 243.

You can also use computer software to create a bar graph with the information from your chart.

INVESTIGATING FURTHER

Graph a Growing Seed

Choose one of the plants that grew from the mung seeds. Measure the height of your plant about five days after it appears above the soil. Continue to measure the height of your plant every five days. Make a graph to show the changes.

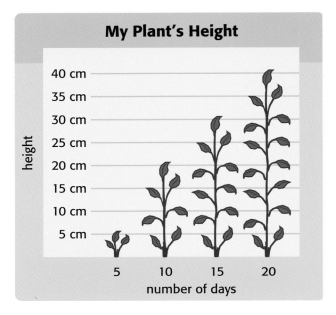

Compare your graph with that of a classmate. How are your graphs the same? How are they different? Why do you think this is so?

Water Power

▼ Percé Rock, Québec

▲ Grand Canyon, United States

Turn on a tap and hold your hand underneath it. What do you feel? Powerful, isn't it? Water can be a mighty force. You can see how powerful water is in rivers, lakes, oceans, and waterfalls. Running water wears away rocks to make river beds and canyons. Water rubs off bits of rock so that they gradually become smaller and smaller. Look at the rocks in these photos. How did the force of water affect their shape?

In **Getting Started** you will talk about how water can move rocks and soil. In **Let's Experiment** you will test how running water affects different types of soil. In **Investigating Further** you can find out about how people stop some of the damage caused by water erosion.

GETTING STARTED

Water can change the shape of rocks. It can also move rocks. How do you think the rocks in this photo got into this valley? Where have you seen water move soil in a similar way?

LET'S EXPERIMENT

You will need
- a lid from a cardboard box such as a shoebox
- a sheet of plastic wrap
- some loam, clay, and sand
- a book
- a plate
- a measuring cup
- water

How does running water affect soil? Watch what happens when water runs down a slope that is covered by three different types of soil.

1. Line the lid of a cardboard box with some plastic wrap.
2. Use a pencil to poke several holes through the plastic and the cardboard in the middle of one end of the lid.
3. Fill the lid with clay soil.
4. Tilt the lid and place the book underneath it so that the lid lies on a slant, with the holes at the lower end. Put the plate under the lower end of the lid.

5. Pour 250 mL of water over the soil.

6. Carefully observe the soil in the lid and the water that collects in the plate. Write your observations in your science journal.

7. Repeat the experiment with the sand and loam soils.

Reflect on Your Results

1. Read what you wrote in your science journal.

2. How did each type of soil look when it was wet?

3. Which sample of collected water had the greatest amount of soil in it?

What Did You Learn?

1. Describe any patterns the water may have left on the soil. Why do you think these patterns appeared?

2. Each time you poured water over the soil, some soil was washed into the plate as well. Think of a reason why this might have happened.

SCIENTISTS IN ACTION

Water that falls on a slope or a hill affects the soil in the same way that it did in your experiment. In the spring, rain and melting snow running down hills can wash away the top layer of soil. This is called water erosion. The top layer of soil is called topsoil. It is usually made up of loam. When it is washed away, plants and crops don't grow as well. Water erosion is a concern for farmers and scientists.

Soil scientists have discovered some ways to stop water erosion. One of the earliest soil scientists was Hugh Hammond Bennett. He grew up on a cotton farm in North Carolina. He is known as the father of soil conservation because he told farmers about ways to save the soil on their farms. Many of his ideas are now used by farmers everywhere.

INVESTIGATING FURTHER

Preventing Erosion

Find out some of the methods farmers are using to prevent erosion. How do they work? Which methods are commonly used in Canada? Which methods are used in other parts of the world?

At Home in the Mud

Some animals use mud and dirt to build their homes. Many birds use mud to build their nests. Beavers use mud to keep water out of their lodges. Perhaps people borrowed the idea from animals of using mud and dirt to build their homes.

In Getting Started you will use a familiar story to help you think about the value of using mud for building a house. In Let's Experiment you will make your own bricks. In Investigating Further you can find out about other animals that dig in the soil to build their homes.

GETTING STARTED

Bricks made out of mud have been used to build homes for thousands of years. Even today, we use soil to make our bricks. Why do you think people want houses made out of brick? why not straw? why not twigs? (Try to remember a particular story.)

LET'S EXPERIMENT

Make your own bricks out of mud.

You will need
- a 500-mL container
- some soil
- water
- pieces of dried grass clippings or straw
- ice-cube trays
- a spoon

1. Put several handfuls of soil into the container.

2. Add enough water to the soil to make a paste.

3. Add some grass or straw.

4. Spoon the mud into the ice-cube trays and place them in the sun, if possible, to dry.

5. Allow enough time for your bricks to set. Empty the bricks out of the ice-cube trays. Describe in your science journal what your bricks look like.

Reflect on Your Results

1. What happened to your soil mixture after you added the grass or straw?

2. How long did it take for your bricks to harden? How could you speed up this part of the experiment?

What Did You Learn?

1. The instructions for making bricks called for straw or grass. Why are they necessary?

2. What would happen if you used only mud to make your bricks?

3. What could you change in the instructions to make a stronger brick?

▲ sod house

▲ adobe bricks

Mud and dirt are cheap building materials and are easy to find. On the Canadian prairie, early settlers built their homes out of sod. They plowed the prairie, and then cut the turned-over sod strips into 1-m lengths. These were placed grass-side down and used like bricks to build the walls of their houses.

In the southwestern United States, Central America, and the Middle East, bricks used to be made out of moulded mud and baked in the sun. The bricks we use today are a modern version of these adobe bricks.

Another way to use earth is in the building of rammed-earth houses. Forms are made for the walls, and then earth is packed down between the forms. Rammed-earth houses are inexpensive since the main ingredient is earth.

▶ This rammed-earth building was constructed in 1826.

INVESTIGATING FURTHER

More Earth Homes

This picture shows a farmer's field. What do you notice about the surface of the soil? Why do you think it looks like this?

Many different animals live under the ground in different types of soil. The marmot lives in a burrow, and the scorpion lives in desert sand. Scientists refer to these animals as subterranean. Why is that a good name for them? (Hint: *Sub-* is the Latin word for "under" and *terranean* comes from *terra*, which means "earth".)

Find out how some animals that live underground use soil for many things besides their homes. Use information resources such as books about animals, encyclopedias, CD-ROMs, and the Internet. How does the soil provide protection for the animals that live underground?

Save Our Earth

By now, you have discovered the important part soil plays in our lives. You have learned how water can both help and harm soil and how plants need organic material in soil to grow. In some areas of the world, the soil has become so polluted with garbage and chemicals that plants can no longer grow in it. Soil needs to be protected from pollution. Soil needs to be taken care of.

It's time to help protect and save our earth. In **Getting Started** you will talk about what our garbage does to soil. In **Let's Investigate** you will track garbage and think of other ways to get rid of it. In **Investigating Further** you can find out more about one way of saving our soil.

GETTING STARTED

Most of our garbage ends up in the ground, in landfills. What can happen to the soil around a landfill? What ways can you think of to prevent garbage from damaging the soil?

LET'S INVESTIGATE

Much of the garbage that ends up in the ground is made up of paper or cardboard. Newspapers are one type of paper. Packaging is another. Track how much paper is thrown out in your home.

1. Make a chart like the one below, or design your own.

Type of paper or cardboard	What was it used for?	How much was there?

2. Set up a box at home to collect all the paper that people throw out.

3. Once a day, look at all the paper being thrown out in your home. List on your chart all the different kinds of paper, including packaging, newspaper, junk mail, and paper towels or tissues.

4. Record your observations on your chart. When you have finished, put the paper in the recycling box or in the garbage.

5. At the end of the week, add up the amount of paper used by your household. Calculate how much paper your household would use in a year.

6. Design a survey for another kind of household waste.

7. Suggest how your household could cut down on the amount of paper used. Which paper products could be eliminated? How? Which paper products could be used differently?

Reflect on Your Results

1. What surprised you most about the results of your investigation?

2. What concerned you about your results?

3. What ways can you think of to make sure that your household's waste paper doesn't end up in a landfill?

What Did You Learn?

1. What did you learn about using resources wisely?

2. How did you use mathematics in this investigation?

3. How was record keeping an important part of this activity?

SCIENCE IN OUR LIVES

On April 22, 1970, the first Earth Day was celebrated. The purpose of Earth Day is to make people aware of the damage being done to the environment.

Canadians across the country participate in Earth Day events every year. These events include planting trees, cleaning up parks, and holding parades, eco-fairs, and workshops.

How is Earth Day celebrated in your school or in your community? Find out and get involved in this year's events.

▲ www.earthday.ca

SCIENTISTS IN ACTION

People who are concerned about what is happening to their world are called environmentalists. One of Canada's environmentalists is Severn Cullis-Suzuki. Severn has a famous father, David Suzuki, who is the host of the TV show called "The Nature of Things". When Severn was nine years old, she travelled to Brazil with her family while her father was filming a program. She became concerned about the damage being done to the rain forests, so she started a group called the Environmental Children's Organization when she got back to Canada. This group travelled to the Earth Summit held in Brazil in 1992. Severn made a speech at that conference that made news around the world. Since then, she has continued to be active in environmental issues.

Severn Cullis-Suzuki has written a book about her work on environmental issues. It's called *Tell the World: A Young Environmentalist Speaks Out* (Doubleday: Toronto, ON, 1993).

There are many Web sites related to Earth Day. Begin your search with the words *Earth Day* and see what you find!

INVESTIGATING FURTHER

Save Our Soil

Use information resources such as books, CD-ROMs, and the Internet, or talk to an expert. Choose one of the following topics to research, or come up with your own.

- reforestation
- strip-cropping
- terracing
- contour plowing
- organic farming
- composting
- reducing, reusing, and recycling

Look for information that explains how the method you are researching prevents soil damage or helps soil to recover from damage. Find out where the method is used. Include any other information you think is important.

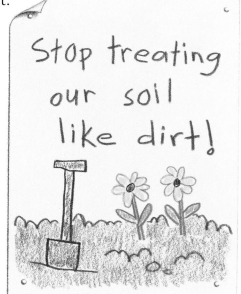

Think about a way to present the information you have found. It could be a poster, a speech, or a school event. Plan your presentation. Include all your information. Prepare your presentation so that it is appealing and attracts attention. Display or perform your presentation for your classmates.

Thinking About Mud and Dirt

1. Draw a picture of a sample of soil. Label all the things that make up soil. How do you know which parts are which?

2. Make up a rhyme or a song that will help you remember three properties of soil.

3. Look at the soil in these photos. What are they called? How do you know?

4. How did your experiment with mung beans show you what type of soil is best for growing plants?

5. What causes mudslides? How could they be prevented?

6. Design an experiment that would test the strength of the mud bricks you made. Remember to include a list of things you will need and a list of steps required to conduct the experiment.

7. How does a survey give us scientific information? What might be a better way to collect information? Why?

Collections

Have you ever collected objects such as rocks, leaves, or feathers? Do you know anyone who collects shells, stamps, or autographs? Collecting things can be a lot of fun.

Collecting objects is an old hobby. Some prehistoric humans collected animal teeth to make into necklaces.

Collections are all around us. Some collections change every day. Others stay the same for many years. In this unit, you will become a collector.

Think about these questions before you begin your collection.

1. Why do people start collections?
2. How do people add to their collections?
3. How do people care for their collections?
4. What are some uses of collections?
5. What kinds of objects do museums collect?

Collector's Corner

Imagine that you collect seeds: big seeds, little seeds, brown seeds, white seeds, flat seeds, round seeds. No matter how different they are, all of the objects in your collection are the same in one important way—they are all seeds.

This is what makes it a collection. All objects in a collection are the same in at least one way, and all objects can be sorted into groups.

CALLING ALL COLLECTORS

Collectors are people who enjoy gathering objects that are similar. Many people begin collecting because it's fun. As they continue to collect, they organize their collections and begin to trade objects with other collectors. This can make collecting very exciting!

Some collections are not meant to be kept. These collections change quickly. Look at the photo below. What kinds of collections can you see? How are they grouped? Why? If the collections were not grouped, what problems might occur?

LEARNING ABOUT COLLECTING

FINDING COLLECTIONS IN SCHOOL

Discover collections in your classroom and in the school.

1. Look for collections of things in your classroom. In your science journal, list any collections that you find.

2. On the map of your school, record two or three of these collections in the space in which your classroom is located.

3. Form a small group with three or four classmates. Choose an area of the school in which to look for collections. Ask for permission and then see what collections you can find there. Record these collections on your school map. Work quietly! You don't want to disturb other students in the school.

You will need
- **a map of your school**

Begin a collector's section in your science journal. Record your ideas about collecting. Include tips from your classmates on starting and keeping a collection.

4. When you return to the classroom, show your map to your classmates. Talk about your discoveries.

5. What collections did you and your classmates find in the library? in the office? in the gym? Mark each collection on your school map.

6. Paste your map in your science journal.

To learn more about collecting, read **_The Young Collector_** by John Hearn (Douglas & McIntyre Ltd., Vancouver, BC, 1983).

FOR YOUR PROJECT

Brainstorming Collections

You are about to become a collector! As a member of a small group, you will build a collection. At the end of the unit, you will display your collection for the rest of the class to view.

Follow these steps to help you decide what to collect.

1. Go for a walk outside with your teacher. Take your science journal with you.

2. Look for objects that you could collect. Record them in your science journal.

3. Return to your classroom. As a class, list objects you could collect, either from your walk or, if you prefer, from home.

4. Write your name and the type of object you would like to collect on a small piece of paper. Give it to your teacher. Your teacher will read your choice and ask you to form a group with two or three other students who want to collect the same type of object.

5. Congratulations! You are now part of an official collectors' group.

IT WORKS! COLLECTIONS

You can become a collector at any age! A four-year-old boy in England began collecting pieces of pottery he found in his parents' garden. He kept his collection in a shoebox. Then the boy began to collect other things. Today, he has a popular museum of farming equipment and tools.

Reflect on Your Results

1. In which area of the school did you find the largest number of collections? Why might this be?

2. A younger student asks you what the word *collection* means. What would you say?

All Eyes!

What makes a good collection great? Perhaps a great collection includes one or two special objects. To find these objects, you—as a collector—need to look carefully at the world around you. You have to observe your world.

CALLING ALL COLLECTORS

Every day, we use our eyes—our sense of sight—to provide us with information about the world around us. Sight is one of five senses. Our other senses are hearing, touch, smell, and taste.

Many people use their sense of sight more than their other senses. By paying more attention to what we see, we can improve our observations. We can learn to see objects in new ways, and we can learn more about events that take place around us.

LEARNING ABOUT COLLECTING

BECOMING A BETTER OBSERVER

Here's your chance to learn something new about an object you wear every day—your shoes!

1. Take off one of your shoes. Draw a picture of it on a piece of paper. Include as many details as you can. Remember, the more you observe, the better your observations will be.

2. On your drawing, write at least five details that describe your shoe. Record more details if you can.

You will need
- one of your shoes

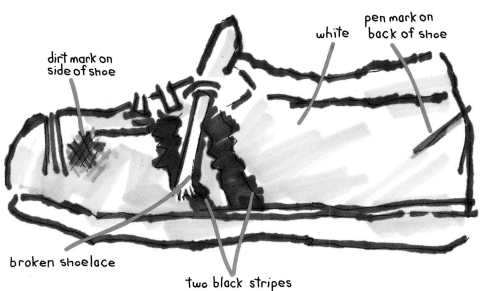

dirt mark on side of shoe

white

pen mark on back of shoe

broken shoelace

two black stripes

3. Sit in a circle with your classmates. Put all the shoe descriptions in a pile. Put one of your shoes in the centre of the circle. Take off your other shoe. Put it behind you so that no one can see it.

4. Take turns choosing a shoe description from the top of the pile and reading it. Listen to each description, then find the shoe that matches it.

You will need
- a large piece of paper
- felt markers, coloured pencils, crayons

FOR YOUR PROJECT

Developing an Action Plan

It's time to develop an action plan. You will need to think about how to begin your collection, how to build it, and how to display it. Here are some questions to get your group started. Write your group's answers to these questions in your science journal.

1. To begin your collection
   - How will you collect objects?
   - How will you decide if an object belongs in your collection?

2. To build your collection
   - How will you bring the objects to class?
   - Where will you store them?

3. To display your collection
   - What do you want people to know about your collection?
   - How can you provide information about your collection?
   - How will you present your collection to others?

4. You and your group will need to include at least six steps in your action plan. Discuss these and other steps.

- decide what to collect
- collect the objects
- examine them and record your observations
- sort the objects into groups
- write descriptions of the objects
- display the collection

Think about what you want your collection to look like. Write about and draw what it will look like in your science journal.

5. Write and illustrate your action plan on a large piece of paper. Print clearly so that others can read your information.

6. Display your plan.

IT WORKS! COLLECTIONS

There are all kinds of collections in the world. Many people collect hockey and baseball cards, rocks, or coins. These are popular objects to collect. Other people like to collect strange objects. There is even a club for people who collect spark plugs (part of a car's engine). Would you like to join this club? Why?

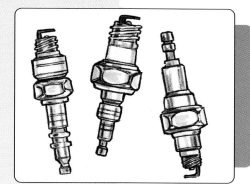

Reflect on Your Results

1. What did you think about as you drew your shoe?

2. When you listened to the shoe descriptions, what kinds of words helped you guess which shoe was being described?

3. Why is it important for scientists to make careful observations and to describe them clearly?

Details, Details, Details

You have learned that as a collector you need to observe your world carefully. Sight is an important sense. Our other four senses also provide us with information about the world. We use our sense of hearing to listen for sounds. We use our sense of smell to tell us about how an object smells—good or bad! We use our sense of touch to discover how an object feels. We use our sense of taste to discover the flavours of what we eat and drink. Imagine a world where you didn't have the use of one of your senses. How would this change the way you live?

LEARNING ABOUT COLLECTING

USING YOUR SENSES TO LEARN

Here's your chance to take a close look at an object you think you know. By using all your senses (except taste), you will learn new facts about the object.

1. Choose one object from your teacher's collection of objects.

2. Look at the object from all sides. What colour (or colours) is the object? How would you describe its shape and size? Would it fit in your hand or would you have to hold it in two hands? Record what you see in your science journal.

3. Pick up the object. How does it feel? Is it smooth? rough? soft? hard? cold? warm? In your science journal, write about how the object feels.

You will need
- a collection of objects
- a measuring tape
- a balance or kitchen scale

Include details in your descriptions. An object may be round, but is it smooth or bumpy? regular or irregular?

4. Hold the object close to your ear. Shake it gently. Does the object make a sound when you shake it? Does the object make a sound when you use it? Record what the object sounds like in your science journal.

5. Hold the object close to your nose. Smell it carefully. Does the object have a smell? Record what the object smells like in your science journal.

6. Use a measuring tape to measure the length and width of your object. Measure the distance around your object, too. Record each measurement in your science journal.

7. Use a balance or a kitchen scale to measure the mass of the object, and record the answer in your science journal.

8. Draw a picture of the object in your science journal. Show as many details as you can.

9. Work with a partner. Compare your object with your partner's (use your science journal to help you). How are they the same? How are they different? Write your answers in your science journal.

To learn how to make your own balance, look on page 240 in the Toolkit.

FOR YOUR PROJECT

Ready, Set, Go!

You have formed a group and you have developed an action plan. Now it's time to begin your collection.

1. Review your action plan with the members of your group.

2. Discuss how you will start gathering objects for your collection.

3. Make sure you have a place in the classroom in which to store your collection.

4. Start collecting!

Reflect on Your Results

1. What new information did you find out about the object when you examined it carefully?

2. Which senses helped you to discover this information?

3. How is using a measuring tape different from using a ruler?

IT WORKS! COLLECTIONS

In the early 1700s, a man in France had a set of buttons made for himself. Each button contained a tiny watch. When other people saw his collection of buttons, they wanted fancy buttons, too. All kinds of materials were used to make buttons, including gold, jewels, wood, and animals' horns. This made some buttons very valuable and people began to collect them. Today, people around the world collect buttons, especially old buttons and buttons that were made by hand.

Sort It Out

One place where you can find many collections is in a museum. Maybe your community has a museum, or you have visited a museum in another town or city. There are many different kinds of museums—art, jewellery, boat, plane, even shoe museums. Most museums, though, display historical objects. These can be objects people once used every day, objects they used only for special purposes, or objects such as documents or drawings. They can also be fossils, or traces left behind by animals or plants that existed long ago.

◀ The Royal Ontario Museum in Toronto, Ontario, is Canada's largest museum.

CALLING ALL COLLECTORS

When you visit a museum, the first thing you may notice is that it contains many collections. For example, a museum may have a collection of dinosaur bones, a collection of farming tools, and a collection of toys.

Objects in each collection have been sorted and are displayed in smaller groups. Remember the seed collection at the beginning of this unit? The seeds could be sorted by colour, size, shape, or weight. Similarly, many large collections are sorted into smaller groups. This makes it easier for people to view and understand the collection.

 **LEARNING ABOUT COLLECTING**

DEVELOPING YOUR SORTING SKILLS

You will need
- a classroom collection
- a large piece of white paper
- felt markers, coloured pencils, crayons

Work in a small group to sort objects in a collection.

1. Form a group with three or four classmates. Together, look at the collection your teacher has given you.

2. Think of ways to sort the collection into groups. You could sort it by colour, shape, texture, size, mass, or type of material.

3. Sort your collection into at least two groups. Then, sort the objects in each group into smaller groups.

4. On a large piece of paper, record how you sorted the objects. You can use pictures or words to show your work.

5. Share your paper with the rest of the class. Check how other groups sorted their collections.

6. Sort your collection in a different way. Ask another group to look at your collection and tell how you sorted it.

Record how your group made decisions about sorting. How difficult was it to decide how your collection should be sorted? Describe how working in a group helps you to understand and learn about the objects in your collection.

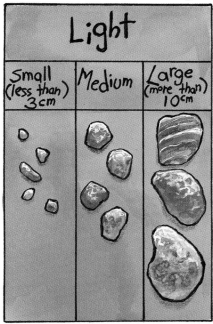

FOR YOUR PROJECT

Organizing Your Collection

Now that you have sorted the collection your teacher gave you, it's time to sort your own collection.

1. Discuss ways to sort your collection. Which ways would make it easiest for someone to view your collection?

2. Make a list of ways to sort your collection.

3. Choose one way of sorting it.

4. Sort objects in each group into smaller groups.

To learn more about collecting and museums, read
Collect It! Making Collections—From Fossils to Fakes
by Elizabeth Newbery
(A & C Black Ltd., London, UK, 1991).

Reflect on Your Results

1. What was the simplest way to sort the collection your teacher gave you? Why?

2. What was the most difficult way to sort the collection? Why?

3. Describe how others were able to decide what sorting rule you used (question 6).

IT WORKS! COLLECTIONS

Many European museums, art galleries, and libraries began as private collections. For example, the British Museum opened because of the work of one man, Sir Hans Sloane. He collected books, fossils, stones, birds, butterflies, and historical objects from around the world. When he died in 1753, the British government decided to display his collection so that everyone could see it. Today, the British Museum is the largest museum in Britain. Each year, it is visited by thousands of people.

Making Scientific Observations

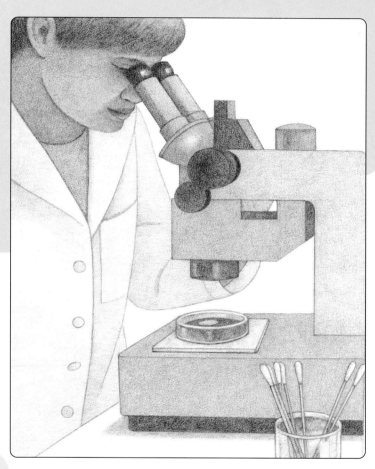

Collectors need good powers of observation. You can use your powers of observation to collect and sort the objects in your collection. You can also use your powers of observation to help you describe the objects in your collection.

Good powers of observation are also important in science. Scientists need to observe objects carefully. Their observations tell them many things: what group an object belongs to, how an object changes when something is added to or taken away from it, and how an object changes on its own.

LEARNING ABOUT COLLECTING

MAKING SCIENTIFIC OBSERVATIONS

You will need
- an object from your teacher
- a measuring tape
- a kitchen scale

Work quietly! Other groups should not know which object you have chosen to work with.

In this activity, you will think like a scientist as you describe an object. You will also discover how much your powers of observation have improved.

1. Form a group with three or four classmates. Your teacher will give you a classroom object to examine.

2. Examine your object. Use your senses of sight, hearing, touch, and smell to learn about it.

3. Record your observations on a piece of paper. Include as many details as you can. Do not include the name of your object.

4. Measure your object. Find its mass and record it.

5. Give your finished list to your teacher. Your teacher will number your list and tell you the number.

6. Choose a list made by another group. Read the group's observations. At the top of the list, write the name of the object you think was described. Give it to your teacher.

7. When everyone has finished, your teacher will read each group's description, tell the class which object the other group thought was being described, and then tell you what the object really was.

IT WORKS! COLLECTIONS

Some scientists work in large museums. Their job is to examine each object in a collection. They identify what the object is made of, where the materials it is made of came from, how it was made, and when it was made. Most of their work is done using powerful microscopes, but sometimes they use other equipment, like X-ray machines, to help them do their job.

FOR YOUR PROJECT

Describing Objects in Your Collection

As a collector, you need to provide information about each object in your collection. One way to do this is to list information on index cards.

You will need
- index cards

Print the information about each object on a piece of paper first. When you are sure it is complete and correct, make a good copy on an index card.

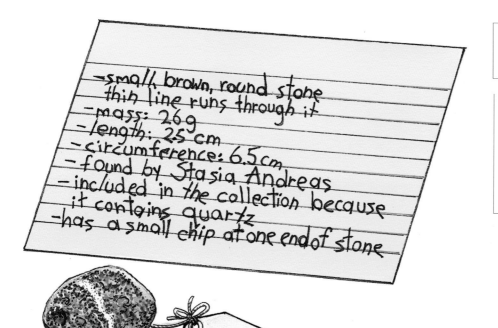

-small, brown, round stone
thin line runs through it
-mass: 26 g
-length: 25 cm
-circumference: 6.5 cm
-found by Stasia Andreas
-included in the collection because
it contains quartz
-has a small chip at one end of stone

Stone #4

Think like a scientist as you work. This will help you make useful observations. Your index cards will be part of your final display, so do your best work.

1. For each object
   - number it
   - draw it (if necessary, label your picture)
   - record three or more observations about it
   - include its mass, length, and the distance around it
   - record who found it
   - record why you included it in the collection
   - record other interesting details

   Print carefully so that others can read your work. Make sure that the number on the index card matches the number of the object it describes.

2. Check your information. Have you included all the details? Add any missing information.

During this project, you have been developing your powers of observation. Describe in your science journal some ways you have become a better observer.

Reflect on Your Results

1. What clues in the description you read helped you guess which object had been described?

2. What important clues did you include in your description that helped others guess the object?

3. Why might it be important to include detailed notes about the objects in a collection?

The Grand Finale

Think back to when you began this project unit. You have learned a lot about how to start and build a collection. You have also learned a lot about making observations and using your observations to write descriptions. Now it's time to look at the final stage of collecting objects—displaying them. Before you make a display for your collection, you need to review what you know about displays.

There are many kinds of displays. Posters, bulletin boards, models, scrapbooks, and exhibits are all examples of displays.

LEARNING ABOUT COLLECTING

EXPLORING DISPLAYS

Here's a chance for you to discover what you know about displays and what makes the difference between a good display and a great display!

1. Form a group with two or three classmates. Look for three displays in the classroom and the school library. For each display, answer these questions in your science journal.

   a) How did the display catch your eye?

   b) How did the presenters use special effects to make their headings stand out?

   c) How is colour used in the display?

   d) How do the pictures help you to understand the text?

   e) What did you learn by reading the display?

   f) What is the best thing about the display?

2. Talk about the displays you examined. What did you like about each one? Write about what you think makes a good display.

3. Together, make a poster about great displays. When you have finished, compare your poster with posters made by other groups.

FOR YOUR PROJECT

Making a Display for Your Collection

The time has come to share your collection with your classmates. Use what you have learned in this unit to help you make an attention-getting display!

1. To display your collection, you will need
   - a background board or poster that tells about your collection
   - something that can be used to display the objects in your collection
   - your index cards
   - a brief biography of each collector (name, age, special interests, experience in collecting)
   - anything else that might be interesting or important

2. Think about the objects in your collection. As a group, choose the best way to display them. Prepare your objects.

3. Decide what information you will include on your background board or poster.

4. Discuss the displays you examined earlier. Brainstorm what you can do to make your display stand out!

5. Prepare your background board.

6. Write your collector biographies.

7. Arrange your display. It should include your background board or poster, the objects in your collection, your index cards, your collector biographies, and anything else you think is important to share with others.

8. Your collection is now ready to be put on display!

> **You will need**
> - poster board
> - felt markers, coloured pencils, crayons
> - your index cards
> - paper
> - a stapler
> - glue
> - scissors
> - other materials of your choice

IT WORKS! COLLECTIONS

Now that you're a collector, you may want to learn more about the objects in your collection. A good place to find information is your school library or your local library. Tell the librarian about your collection and the information you are looking for. The librarian may be able to help you find books about the objects you are collecting. Some objects are so popular that there are special magazines for collectors and clubs collectors can join. You may also find information about the objects in your collection on the Internet. Ask the librarian to help you to do a search.

What Did You Learn?

1. What did you learn about great displays?

2. What did other groups do in their displays that you might do next time? What was good about their idea(s)? Why?

Thinking About Collections

1. What interesting or surprising things did you learn about the objects you collected by observing them carefully?

2. Think of one collection of objects in your home or at school. How are the objects grouped? How does grouping the objects help people understand the collection?

3. Is a garden a collection? Why or why not?

4. How did working as a team help you gather, organize, and display your collection?

5. What do you think you might collect next? How will you begin your collection?

6. Imagine that someone asks you for advice on how to start a collection. Think about what you have learned during this unit. What would you tell this person?

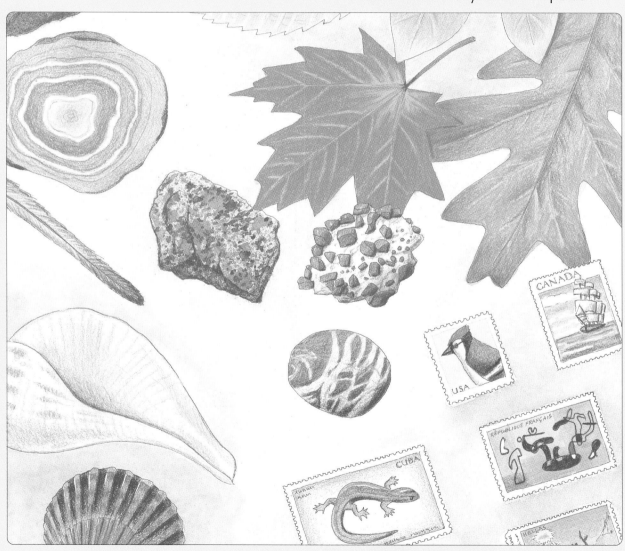

Celebrating Science

Throughout the year you learned many things about science and technology. You will be able to use the information you have learned and the skills you have developed in many ways.

To celebrate your learning, you are going to work as part of a team, practising for the Science Everywhere Games. Later in this unit you will make up your own events for the Science Everywhere Games.

Jump To It!

What happens when you pull a sweater on over your head? When certain types of materials are rubbed together, they become electrically charged. We call this static electricity.

In Getting Started you will think of ways static electricity affects you. In Let's Investigate you will observe how static electricity affects different materials.

GETTING STARTED

When has static electricity happened to you? Where else have you seen static electricity? How can you tell when static is there?

LET'S INVESTIGATE

Find out about static electricity.

You will need
- small pieces of different materials (lined paper, aluminum foil, cardboard, tissue paper, cloth, plastic foam)
- a plastic comb
- a piece of wool

1. Place small pieces of paper on your desk.

2. Rub the piece of wool over the comb several times.

3. Move the comb close to the paper. What happens?

4. Repeat steps 1 to 3 using different materials.

5. Write your observations in your science journal.

Reflect on Your Results

1. Why do you think the pieces of paper moved?

2. What other materials were attracted to the comb?

3. Write a sentence in your science journal telling what you discovered about static electricity.

4. Read the Information Station to learn about static electricity and why it happens.

INFORMATION STATION

Opposites Attract

All materials are made of tiny particles that have electric charges. Some of these electric charges are positive and others are negative. Normally the positive and negative charges balance each other. When you rub a comb with a piece of wool, tiny negative particles move from one object to the other, leaving both with an electric charge.

Electrically charged objects are able to attract things around them that have an opposite charge. They also repel things that have the same charge. Rubbing wool over a plastic comb gives it a negative charge. As you bring the comb close to the pieces of paper, which have no charge, the negative charges in the comb repel the negative charges in the pieces of paper, exposing the positive charges. The positive charges in the paper are attracted to the negative charges in the comb and the pieces of paper follow the comb.

What Did You Learn?

1. Describe how you could use a balloon, a woolen sock, and a wall to show how static electricity works.

SCIENTISTS IN ACTION

Thousands of years ago a man named Thales of Miletus discovered static electricity. After polishing an amber stone with a cloth, he noticed that dust and pieces of cloth were attracted to the stone. The word *electricity* comes from the Greek word for amber, *elektron*.

INVESTIGATING FURTHER

Invisible Power

Make a table-tennis ball follow you using a comb and a piece of wool. What did you do? See how far you can make the table-tennis ball travel to the comb. Have a race with a classmate. See who can make the table-tennis ball travel the farthest.

A Sticky Situation

Believe it or not, the questions in the pictures below have something in common. Both of them are about static electricity.

In **Getting Started** you will discuss with a partner when you have seen or have felt static electricity. In **Let's Investigate** you will get to see static electricity in action.

Why does the TV screen get so dusty?

Why do these socks always stick together?

GETTING STARTED

Work with a partner. Discuss when you have seen or felt static electricity. Share your ideas with the class.

LET'S INVESTIGATE

These activities will give you some more chances to see static electricity in action.

Work with a partner. How can you use the materials at each station to make a static charge?

Read the instructions at each station and then try them. Write the rules you used for each station in your science journal. Decide how successful you were.

STATION A: STICKING BALLOON

Try to get a balloon to stick to a wall. How long can you keep the balloon stuck to the wall?

STATION B: MOVING BALLOON

Try to use a balloon to move a balloon that is hanging from a thread. How far can you make the balloon move?

STATION C: BENDING WATER

Try to bend a stream of water using a balloon. How can you remove static from the balloon?

Reflect on Your Results

1. Look at the rules you wrote for each event. Explain why each rule is necessary for making a fair test.
2. Share your ideas with another pair of students for removing static from a balloon.

You will need

Station A
- inflated balloons
- pieces of different fabrics
- a timer

Station B
- inflated balloons
- thread
- a ruler

Station C
- inflated balloons
- water
- a cup
- a basin

What Did You Learn?

1. What did you do at each station to make a static charge?

2. List ways a static charge can be removed.

3. Read Science in Our Lives to find out more about static electricity and electric charges.

SCIENCE IN OUR LIVES

When a balloon is rubbed with wool or some other fabrics, the wool or fabrics make part of the balloon negatively charged even though the rest of the balloon may remain uncharged. When you place the balloon on a wall, the negative charges in the balloon repel the negative charges in the wall, exposing the positive charges. The negative charges in the balloon are attracted to the positive charges in the wall.

Every water particle has one end that is a bit positive and one end that is a bit negative because of the way it is put together. As water falls from a tap, the negative charges on the balloon attract the positive charges in the water. What would happen if you brought a charged balloon close to a sink full of water? Will you get the same result? Try it and find out.

Planning Your Event

WELCOME TO THE SCIENCE EVERYWHERE GAMES!

You have learned many things about science and technology this year. You will be able to use the information you have learned and the skills you have developed. To celebrate your learning, you are going to work as a member of a team to create an event for the Science Everywhere Games.

In **Getting Started** you will review what you've learned throughout the year. In **Let's Plan** you and your classmates will discuss all the things you've learned and done this year. In **Let's Design** you will use what you've learned this year to design an event for the Science Everywhere Games.

GETTING STARTED

Take a few minutes to read your science journal. Look through this book, too.

What are some of the things you did? What are some of the things you learned? Write your observations in a chart like this one.

A Review of Science Everywhere	
Things we did	Things we learned
We picked up paper clips with a magnet	Magnets pick up things that have iron in them.

LET'S PLAN

What a lot of learning you have done!

You can celebrate what you have learned by holding the Science Everywhere Games. You will work in groups of three or four, planning events for your Science Everywhere Games. Each group will make up one event.

In the first two learning events you learned about static electricity. All of the activities could be events held at the Science Everywhere Games. As a group decide what you would like to celebrate with your event.

1. Read the lists that people in your group made of things they learned.

2. Ask each person in your group to suggest two possible things to celebrate that they learned.

3. As a group decide what your whole group would like to celebrate.

4. Decide together what two things you could ask your classmates to do.

LET'S DESIGN

Before holding an event in the Science Everywhere Games, you'll need to write the instructions and rules for your event, as well as any materials you will need. Follow these steps for designing your event.

1. Describe an activity that you think will be a good challenge.

2. List the materials you will need. Make sure these materials are easy to find. Gather them.

3. Test your idea to make sure it works.

4. Write instructions and rules for your event.

5. Give your event a title or name.

List three things that make instructions easy to follow.

1. Why is it important to test your event before the Science Everywhere Games are held?

2. How difficult might it be to follow your instructions and the rules for your event? Why?

3. If you can't find some of the materials you listed, what could you use instead?

4. In what ways did your group work together as a team?

5. How does working in a group make developing an event easier? more difficult?

The Science Everywhere Games

The time has come to hold the Science Everywhere Games.

In Getting Started you will think about ways to have successful Science Everywhere Games. In Let's Celebrate you will hold your Science Everywhere Games event. Have fun!

GETTING STARTED

Talk with a partner about what will be needed to make the Science Everywhere Games a success. Will you need a signal to move from one event to another? What else will you need? Share your ideas with the class.

LET'S CELEBRATE!

You will need
- **the materials necessary to complete each event**

For each event you will need one person to read the instructions, one to check that all the materials are in place, and another person to record your results.

1. Place the materials for your group's events at a station.
2. Start at a station that another group has set up.
3. Follow the instructions to complete that event.
4. Record your results in your science journal.
5. Move to another station and repeat steps 3 and 4.

Reflect on Your Results

1. As a group, choose one event to discuss.
2. How successful were you at this event?
3. What made the instructions for the event easy to follow? What did you have trouble with?
4. At which event were your results different from what you expected them to be? Why do you think this happened?
5. What science and technology did you learn by making your event?
6. What science and technology did you learn by participating in other groups' events?

Toolkit

MAKING A MAGNIFIER

1. Fill your jar with water.
2. Put the lid on tightly so no water can leak out.
3. Turn the jar on its side and place it on an open book or newspaper.
4. Look through your magnifier. How does it change what you see?
5. Move the jar a little bit away from the paper. Move it close again. How does moving the jar change what you see?

MAKING A BALANCE

1. Bend each paper clip open so it looks like this.

2. Open the plastic bags. Push one end of each paper clip through one side of each plastic bag near the top corner.

3. Hook the other end of each paper clip over an end of the hanger. Tape the paper clips onto the hanger.

4. Hang the hanger on a doorknob.

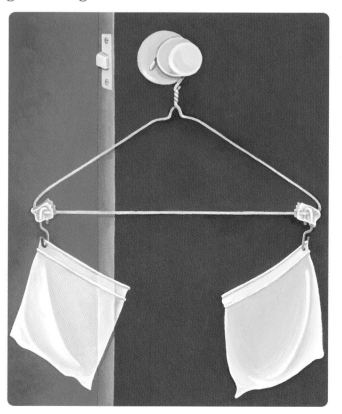

You can put things into each bag to compare their mass. The heaviest thing will pull its side of the hanger down.

USING TOOLS

These tools can help you build things:

- safety glasses
- drill
- saw with fine teeth
- mitre box
- screwdrivers
- screws
- small claw hammer
- nails
- clamps

These tools can help you take things apart:

- safety glasses
- needle-nose pliers
- adjustable wrench
- screwdrivers
- vise

These rules can keep you safe when you build things or take them apart:

- Always wear safety glasses.
- Work away from others so you won't hit them with your tools by accident.
- Use tools only for the jobs they were meant to do.
- Take your time—don't rush.
- Keep your work space clean and tidy.
- Put tools away after you have used them.

PULLER PAL

A puller pal is a tool that will help you measure how hard you are pulling.

1. Loop the elastic band through the large paper clip.

2. Attach the large paper clip to one end of the ruler.

3. Loop the other end of the elastic band through the small paper clip.

4. Cut a piece of string 30 cm long.

5. Tie one end of the string to the small paper clip and the other end to the binder clip.

6. Attach the binder clip to the object you need to pull.

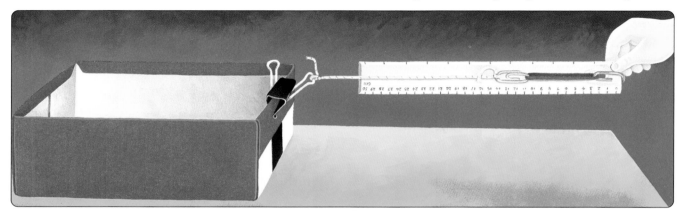

To what number on the ruler does the small paper clip move when you pull a light load? To what number on the ruler does the small paper clip move when you pull a heavy load? The higher the number on the ruler that the small paper clip reaches, the more force you are using to pull the load.

MAKING A PICTOGRAPH

A pictograph can help you compare numbers of things. If you ask people what their favourite fruit is, you might get these results. You can use a pictograph to explain the results.

Fruit	Number of people
apples	3
blueberries	4
pears	2
strawberries	5

1. Draw a long line near the bottom of a piece of paper.

2. Below the line, write the names of the fruits.

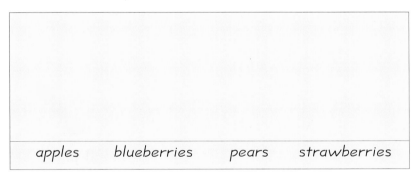

3. For every person who said they liked apples best, draw a face above the word "apples". Do the same for the other fruits.

4. Give your pictograph a title.

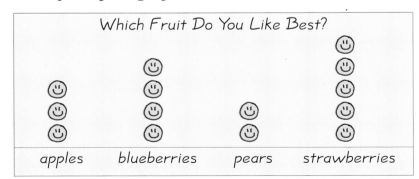

How does your pictograph help you see which fruit most people liked best?

GATHERING INFORMATION

You can learn about a topic in many ways. One way is to find a book about it.

Libraries have many books. Use these tips to find the books that will help you the most.

1. Choose key words that really describe what you want to learn. Use them to search for books. To look for books about growing vegetables use the words "vegetable gardening". If you just use the word "gardening" you will find books that don't say anything about vegetables. If you just use the word "vegetables" you will find mostly cookbooks.

2. Check the table of contents of a book to see if it does have information that will help you.

3. Turn to a page about your topic. Read two or three sentences. If you can understand what you read, the book might help you. If you have trouble understanding it, choose another book.

There are other ways to learn about a topic. You could try

- looking on a CD-ROM or on the Internet (Ask an adult to help you.)
- interviewing someone who knows about the topic
- writing a letter to an expert to ask for information

Acknowledgements

Photographs

T = top, C = Centre, B = Bottom, L = Left, R = Right

p. 12: (l) Dick Hemingway, (tr) A. Bartel/Science Photo Library/Publiphoto, (br) M. Yamashita/Corbis; 15: L.S. Stepanowicz/Visuals Unlimited; 30: Orion/Spectrum/Ivy Images; 33: (t) S. Bennett/Spectrum/Ivy Images, (b) M. Beedell/Ivy Images; 41: (t) Dick Hemingway, (b) B. Chambers/Spectrum/Ivy Images; 51: F. Scott/Spectrum/Ivy Images; 53: B. Ivy/Ivy Images; 62: (t) B. Ivy/Ivy Images, (b) P. Bissett/Spectrum/Ivy Images; 70: (bl) D. Wiggett/First Light, (tl) T. Kitchin/First Light, (r) S. Vidler/Comstock; 83: Spectrum/Ivy Images; 95: D. Roitner/Spectrum/Ivy Images; 98: Design and construction management by Chamberlain Architect Services Limited, Burlington, Ontario; 101: Design and construction management by Chamberlain Architect Services Limited, Burlington, Ontario/Photo by Bochsler Photographics+ Imaging, Burlington, Ontario; 103: L. Lee/First Light; 107: H. Armstrong Roberts/Comstock; 110: S. Vidler/Comstock; 112: First Light; 123: (t) D. McCoy/Rainbow, (b) The Granger Collection, New York; 136: (bl) F. Lepine/Valan Photos, (tl) J.A. Wilkinson/Valan Photos, (r) J. Sohlden/Visuals Unlimited; 151: (t, b) NASA; 161: (l) P. Carpentier/Publiphoto, (r) B. Ross/First Light, (b) M. Meadows/Peter Arnold, Inc.; 164: (t) M. Berkman/Publiphoto, (b) P.G. Adam/Publiphoto; 170: (t) First Light, (b) V. Last/Geographical Visual Aids; 174: V. Last/Geographical Visual Aids; 181: (t) V. Last/Geographical Visual Aids, (b) Kitchin & Hurst/First Light; 182: P.G. Adam/Publiphoto; 184: A.S. MacLean/Peter Arnold, Inc.; 188: CSIRA Bulletin; 190: A. Masson/Publiphoto; 193: Courtesy Earth Day Canada; 195: (bl) S.J. Krasemann/Peter Arnold, Inc., (tl) T. Campbell/First Light, (r) F. Dumouchel/Publiphoto; 199: B. Wittman/Comstock; 210: Dick Hemingway; 211: Copyright Royal Ontario Museum, Toronto, Ontario; 214: B. Rondel/First Light.

Illustrations

Dorothy Siemens: pp. 3 (left), 4 (right), 26-27, 31, 34, 36, 38, 39, 42, 46, 48, 50, 55, 56, 58, 60, 64, 67, 196-97, 198, 223; John Fraser: pp. 3 (right), 9, 127, 133, 141, 156, 159, 165, 171, 172, 173, 179, 194; Michael Dixon: pp. 4 (left), 157, 162, 167, 183, 185, 186, 189; Heather Graham: pp. 6-7, 17, 19, 72, 100, 105, 109, 148, 149, 202, 215; William Kimber: pp. 8, 32, 45, 49, 63, 65, 86, 89, 95, 114, 129, 130, 137, 146, 153; Henry Van Der Linde: pp. 11, 22, 25, 28, 29, 30, 35, 40, 54, 61, 79, 84, 88, 92, 93, 94, 96, 131, 138, 143, 144, 203, 205, 213, 217, 219; Stephen Taylor: pp. 13, 16, 18, 23, 145, 207, 208, 227, 230 (left); Jock MacRae: pp. 21, 74, 76, 80, 85, 132, 140; Carl Wiens: pp. 44, 119; Chrissie and David Wysotski: pp. 68-69, 111; Greg Douglas: pp. 71, 78, 87, 222; Drew-Brook-Cormack: pp. 75, 91, 97, 115, 124, 128, 235, 237; Malcolm Cullen: pp. 118, 121, 122, 125, 150; Sarah Jane English: pp. 154-55, 188; Deborah Crowle: pp. 169 (map), 180; Annette Tavares-Cromar: pp. 176, 178; Patty Gallinger: pp. 200; Steve Schulman: pp. 201, 206, 216; June Lawrason: pp. 224-25; Michele Nidenoff: pp. 226, 230 (right), 232, 233, 239, 240, 242.

The authors and publisher would like to thank the following teachers and their students for helping with the development of *Science Everywhere*:

Sue Voll, N. A. MacEachern Public School, Ontario

Pat Campbell, Howard Debeck Elementary School, British Columbia

Jill Detrubide, Michael Wallace Elementary School, Nova Scotia

Lucille Edmundson, Dougall Avenue Public School, Ontario

Terry Forster, Howard Debeck Elementary School, British Columbia

Mary Helen Harrigan, Holy Rosary School, Ontario

Jeff Hillman, Southwood Public School, Ontario

Pat Liffiton, Dougall Avenue Public School, Ontario

Lilli Kenna, Franklin Public School, Ontario

Brenda MacNeil, Michael Wallace Elementary School, Nova Scotia

Wayne Minick, Baden Public School, Ontario

Joyce Tremaine, Dr. Taylor Elementary School, Ontario

Sherry Weese, Gordon McGregor Elementary School, Ontario